Day 1: Rome

It took almost an hour to get immigration after landing in Rome! Two Japanese girls sat in front of me and I spoke to them. They were there visiting their friends. After I had cleared immigration, I took Leonardo Express to Termini Station. It was already close to 30 degrees, even though it was only 9:30 AM. Rome was hotter than I remember. I asked a young man at Termini Station for directions to my hotel. He used Google Map to show me how to get there. The young man helped me find my hotel and I was able to get there without any difficulty!

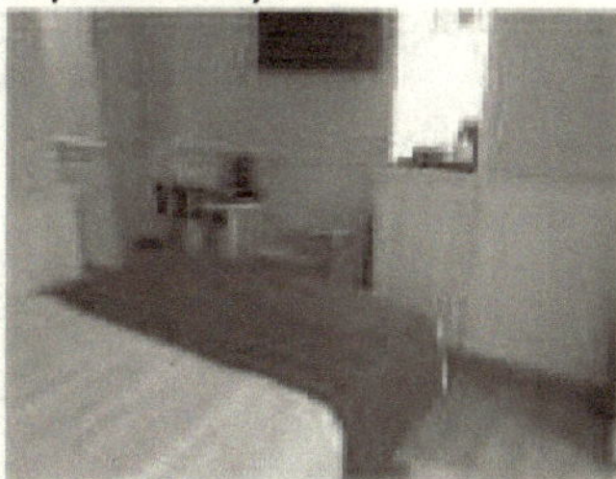

When I arrived, my room was ready for me. After grabbing some fruit and an egg from the breakfast bar, I snoozed for approximately half an hour. Although the room was small, it was very clean and beautiful. It overlooked a peaceful courtyard. After a nap, I went for a walk. Basilica di Santa Maria Maggiore was the first church I visited. It was stunning inside and out. It was still very hot. As soon as I left the hotel, I regretted my decision. It wasn't the best hour to go sightseeing at noon. After the service, I went to Termini Station to shop for a blouse in Sisley and two dresses in Benetton.

I was lost on my return trip, but a friendly man across the street helped me find my way. I got a gelato from the station. It was dark chocolate with coconut. Italians are masters at making ice cream. After I returned to the hotel, I took another nap for nearly an hour. I was tired. I then updated my journal, and was ready to go for the opera tonight.

Eugene picked me-up around 5pm. Eugene was an old friend of mine in Tokyo when I lived there. He didn't ride his motorcycle, which was a great thing! Hospitals are not exciting enough for some doctors, evidently. He said he would ride his bike. I was shocked. I explained to him that I would be wearing an evening dress and that we were going on a picnic, not an opera. He finally got it. Men!

Eugene arrived at my hotel to find that a protest was about start near my hotel. They were already preparing for the protest this morning, and police officers were all around. When I checked in to the hotel that morning, I was puzzled as to why so many policemen were there. According to reports, around 20 people were killed in another protest against refugees the week prior. They now wanted to make it more peaceful. I was happy that I did not live in Europe. Eugene's plans to move is not something I blame!

Eugene was very pleased with the little restaurant he booked. It was delicious! Each appetiser was delicious and I couldn't help but eat more. Although the mushroom pasta was spicy, I loved it. Although the clam pasta with white wines was delicious, I found the pasta a little too dense for my liking. He was also a fantastic musician! His vocal range was amazing and he sang both English and Italian songs. His rendition of "human saxophone" was a delight. He sang a western cowboy song with only his vocal skills, and then he sang an operatic song with a female voice. It was very entertaining!

We walked to the theatre after dinner - which was a mistake! After 10 minutes of walking along the cobblestone streets, I developed a blister the first day of my holiday! But I was so excited for the show, that I chose to ignore the pain. Eugene took a picture of me in front a fountain. An American girl approached me and asked if she could take photos of me. I reluctantly agreed. It was difficult for me to accept it. Eugene later explained that I was most likely like an UNESCO site. What? In my decayed glory?

The opera was a success. They were two of the most talented Alfredo and Violet singers I've ever heard. If they were born in New Zealand, they would have been a national treasure. They performed in Italy for tourists. All the top NZ musicians travel to Europe, and only the very best stay there.

However, the orchestra tonight needed to practice more individually and together, but it was a great show. La Traviata was a favorite of mine growing up. I know all the songs and the story, but tonight's performance brought me to tears. Eugene dropped me off at my hotel a few minutes later. Although I was tired, I was still buzzing from the opera!

Day 2: Rome

The next day, I was jet-lagged. But I was determined to stay awake, and shopping was the only way I could do that. So I took a taxi to Zara's flagship store on Plaza Cologne. Shopping in Rome is my favorite place to shop! It was also a great place to take your dog! !

I began sightseeing in the afternoon. The Coloseum was my first stop, but I was too afraid to go in. When I went back, I cried like an infant. I then went to Plaza Novana, and the Pantheon. Tourists were everywhere! According to me, most Romans were on vacation because of the heat.

Next, I visited Plaza Venezia and Trevi Fountain. Although I've been to these places before, I was still fascinated 11 years ago!

Although it was getting dark, I wanted to go back to the Spanish Steps. The sun was setting when I finally reached the Spanish Steps.

I was nearly nine o'clock when I returned to the hotel. The Basilica di Santa Maria Maggiore was spectacularly lit in the darkness.

Later, I had dinner at a restaurant recommended by my hotel. It was the best pizza I have ever had in Rome!

Saluti!

Day 3: Florence

I booked business class. It was 44 euros and took approximately 1.5 hours. It was extremely comfortable. It was a beautiful view of the countryside. To find my hotel, it took me nearly half an hour. By then, I was totally melted. My blister was sore and it felt like it was over 40 degrees. Nearly crying when the hotel asked me to return in 1.5 hours as my room was not ready!

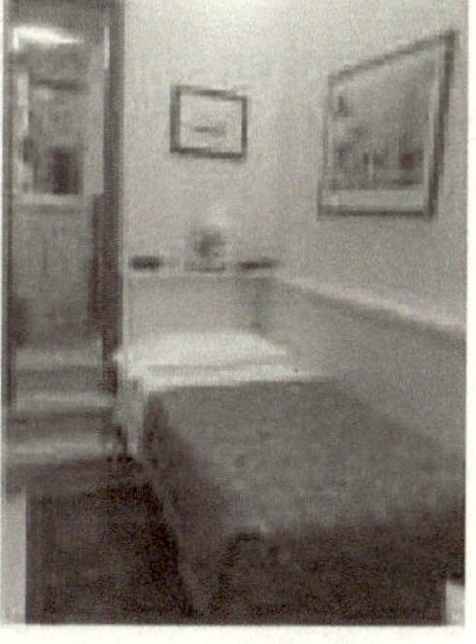

I washed my clothes and took my bag with me. Then, I reluctantly returned to the heat. The Medici Palace was the first place I visited. A Chinese art exhibit was on display. Although I was intrigued, I didn't make it all the way to Florence just to see Chinese art.

Florence is home to the most beautiful duomo! Nearly half an hour later, I was still there and asked nearly 10 people to take photos for me. This is the best shot. Although the young girl who took it seemed a bit nerdy, she was an excellent photographer. It wasn't her fault... I was unable to find my way back into the hotel later. This heat was not enjoyable!

Google Maps app helped me find my way back to the hotel. It was wonderful!

My room was ready at 1pm. Phew! It was small and very basic. Florence hotels can be very expensive. This hotel was chosen because of its central location.

After that, I went to Central Market for lunch. It was delicious! This dish even had a Japanese sign! It was cool and comfortable inside because the market had air conditioning. In case I needed to sleep again, I bought a small bottle of Chianti. I then went to Lorenzo Market. The quality of the products there was not very good, so I settled for a regular shop. I bought four leather pouches as presents. I nearly bought a pair red gloves with black dots, but they were too bulky to be worn outside of the bedroom!

Day 4: Florence

Around 9 a.m., I began exploring the city. Florence was still waking up, but there were already quite some tourists around, probably jetlagged like I! Although the wine truck looked great, I was probably craving coffee!

Although some of the jewellery shops at Ponte Vecchio were just opening, most of them were still asleep. I was able to cross the bridge without purchasing any bling bling. I'm so proud of myself!

Piazza della Sognoria was crowded with tourists. It was hard to take a picture of David without anyone else.

Later, I went on the Secrets of Inferno Tour at Palazzo Vecchio. I was the only person on the tour, so Stefano, my knowledgeable guide, was all mine.

Cosimo deMedici displayed his wealth and power in the '500 People Room. There were many paintings that depicted wars. I felt that Florence was built from piles upon piles of bodies.

Stefano took me upstairs so I could see the ceiling where the female assassin from the movie fell through. All of the scenes were done by CG. They didn't intend to cut the ceiling. However, they did rent the palace for one week. We then went to the Map Room, where Tom Hanks discovered the secret way to escape.

Every detail in the palace is exquisite, from the ceilings to the furniture and paintings to the sculptures. The palace's main purpose was to display the wealth and power of the family. Although the actual living space was small, it was spacious and beautiful. We had finally a medieval fashion show. Do I look like one those "men in tights?"?

After the tour, we went to Central Market where we bought lunch and dinner. I also bought 3 pairs gloves from the market outside on my return.

As I was returning to my hotel, I noticed some soldiers guarding Duomo. It was a great feeling to be in Europe. A terrorist attack took place just a few weeks ago. What will happen next?

Day 5: Venice

Venice was just as beautiful as I remembered it to be! It took me over 30 minutes to board the water taxi. Some locals skipped the queue. Finally, an American girl stopped them. Bravo!

Water is the secret to Venice's charm. Everything shines here! It is difficult to take bad photos in Venice. On my way, I came across the Rialto Bridge.

To get to Piazza San Marko took approximately 20 minutes. It was just as crowded as I remembered!

I followed the hotel's website directions and went to this arcade, but it was incorrect. After 5 people had given me incorrect directions, it was nearly an hour later that I couldn't find my hotel despite having a GPS, a map, and the hotel directions. I finally found someone who knew the hotel and not just guessing. It was hidden behind a gate in a quiet courtyard. It was well hidden behind a gate in a courtyard.

The hotel was a former palace. It even had its very own swimming pool.

boarding deck! Every room in this hotel was given a name and not a number. It was very classy! I felt like royalty! !

After taking a break, I began exploring. It's easy to get used to getting lost once you learn how. I just adore it!

I saw the same person who had accompanied me to my hotel earlier on my return trip. He was a waiter at a nearby restaurant. I was still hungry so I went to the restaurant for an early dinner. The crayfish pasta was delicious and it cost me only 45 Euros. For dessert, I had gelato!

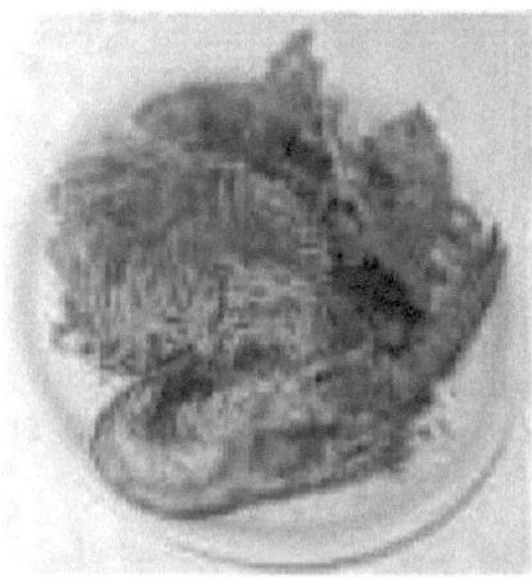

It was getting darker outside. The concert began at 9pm. It took me an hour to locate the venue, even though it was only 10 minutes away!

I began to worry after about 40 minutes. I couldn't find my way... Luckily, I met a couple from England who were also looking for Church of San Vidal. They were both going to the same concert!

Vivaldi was born in Venice. It seemed fitting to hear his music in Venice. It was a tiny church with a magnificent interior! There were five violinists, one cellist, and one double bassist. The musicians played mostly Vivaldi, with the exception of one piece by Bartok.

Although the musicians were great, the first violinist was too young to be able to play in their encore. Even though he was technically brilliant, he had a lot of trouble communicating his emotions. It is my belief that you can't make others feel it if you don’t feel it. On the other hand, the cellist was playing his heart out!

After the concert, I walked with the British couple back to Piazza San Marco.

With its lights on, the palace looked magnificent.

Day 6: Venice

This was my favorite bed on the trip. I was so tired from the last night that I didn't get to sleep until midnight, and it wasn't long before I had to go to bed. My room was also a delight. The room had 5 mirrors, and the chandelier was amazing!

It was also my favorite breakfast I have ever had! The breakfast was prepared fresh to order. I also found a heart in my cup of coffee!

I tried on a famous Venetian mask while walking to the Basilica skip-the-line entry. I eventually purchased one. Although the Basilica's interior was not as impressive as the facade, I was happy to be able to enter the Basilica without waiting in the long queue like many people. Minori, another solo traveller, was also there. Just like me, she taught at a Japanese university. We began to speak Japanese. We took photos together, then I told her all about the concert and she said that she would be there.

Later, I went for a stroll around the area. It was just before 10am, and the plaza was crowded with tourists.

In the courtyard, began the Secret Itinerary Tour of Dodge's Palace. We were around 30 people. It is simply breathtaking!

We also saw The Bridge of Sighs. Casanova was fortunate to escape! The prison was not something I enjoyed. The darkest sides of humanity were revealed during our tour.

I stopped by a Chinese restaurant for lunch after the tour. It was amazing how much I missed Asian food! Beef noodles and silk melons. Yum!! After a quick nap, Lorenzo at front desk printed my boarding pass. He was great! Gigi was also a tremendous help. He organized the water taxi from the airport to my home for me this morning. He was efficient and friendly. Later, I walked to the concert venue. Following Lorenza's directions was simple. I was on my way and asked a man for directions to the concert venue. He said he would take me there later. He was done with work by 7:15pm. Italian men excel at flirting!

It was almost unbearably warm. I had to have a gelato. One gelato per day keeps the doctor away I asked a man to take a picture of me, and later he took a selfie with my face. I returned to the hotel and updated our journal.

Minori was not there when I arrived at the venue at 7:05pm. After waiting a while, I asked them to take photos of me and the man in costume. The middle-aged Italian man who was our photographer told the young man to get closer to me. You Italian men! To kill some time, I later went to Pandora near my home and bought a diamond! Roldolfo came to meet me as I was waiting in line for the concert. When he saw me waiting in line for the concert, he asked where I was from. He started speaking in Japanese, but he switched to English later.

He is originally from Canada and works as a lecturer in Japan.

Minori arrived at 7:40pm, and she was not happy. I was still waiting for her.

San Marco Plaza! She misunderstood what I said and she went to the wrong place. Eimi and Saleh sat beside Roldolfo (my seat was in another area) as we all sat down to the concert. Eimi is half Japanese and half American. They also started speaking Japanese!

It was a great concert. The little guy to the left had a great vocal range and was an excellent actor. Although he had a funny face, he sang the Alfredo song to Violet about his daughter with a beautiful and effortless voice. It was a far better performance than the one at La Traviata, Rome, the other night.

After the concert, everyone went to San Marco Plaza for drinks. It was our last night in Venice. The band was playing, and five of our new friends laughed. It was an unforgettable evening celebrating friendship. Although there are many interactions in our lives, only a few stand out. It's amazing that I was able to meet all four of them in one day. People are the reason I travel.

Day 7: Vienna

Around 5:30 AM, I was woken by a thunderstorm. The rain started pouring and the sky opened up! I got up and started to get dressed. I took my time getting ready, and checked out at 7:30 am. For breakfast, I ordered an omelette. Yum! I sat down at the table by the canal. Gigi, the receptionist / coowner, came over to have a chat. I learned that his real name was Luigi Segatto, and that he used to be an Alitalia flight attendant.

After breakfast, I returned to my hotel room to write a glowing review and then got ready to take my water taxi to the airport. I was accompanied by a couple from Sweden in the taxi. The taxi stopped right outside our hotel. That was so cool! We were driven by the taxi driver to the airport. I was very nervous when he stopped the taxi to make sure there wasn't any noise behind him. He delivered us all to the airport in 20 minutes. It was an exciting start to the day. On the way, I thought "hmmm... I wish I remembered how to swim!

My flight was delayed by 40 minutes, so I had no choice but to postpone my afternoon tour until the morning. According to the weather forecast, it was going rain in Vienna today so I decided to move the tour to tomorrow. After waiting in line for around half an hour, the boarding process began. The group piled onto a bus, and then waited for everyone to get on. Finally, we boarded the plane. Although it took us only 50 minutes to get from Venice to Vienna, they still offered snacks and beverages. The uniforms of flight attendants were a delight!

I purchased my CAT ticket from Vienna airport and collected my ticket.

Vienna Pass. The train reached Wien Central after 16 minutes. I switched to Line 4 at the second station. I was unable to turn on my mobile data at the station so I went to information and asked for directions. It was easy. I found my hotel in 5 minutes. It was pouring outside.

It was already 2 p.m. when I checked in. After leaving my bag in the room, I decided to go out for lunch at the Asian restaurant nearby. Although the staff was not friendly, the food was excellent! I tried to nap after lunch but the children next door were screaming. I asked for an upgrade at reception. I was able to find a room, which was their last one, and it was available. It didn't have a bathtub and it was 25 euros more per night, but I chose to use it. I needed to get some sleep. The new room had a bedroom for four people. It was a complete apartment. The entrance had a hallway. It was amazing!

Although it was only a brief nap, I did finally get my rest. Then, I went to the grocery store to buy dental floss and a bandage for my blister. It was located in the basement of a mall just a block away. It was rainy and cold, almost like Auckland. I was able to find my dental floss, but couldn't find any bandages rolls. There were also clothes shops. Although I didn't spend too much time shopping, I did find a cute blouse at half price so I bought it.

There was a huge selection of chocolates in the supermarket. The pretty floral ones were my favorite. I bought 3 boxes of mangos, a fresh bottle of red current juice, chips, nuts and a muffin to make tomorrow's breakfast.

I returned home and watched CNN, the only English Channel that they had. I also had a light dinner in our room. I fell asleep at 8:30pm and realized how tired I was. I had done far too much in the first week. I needed to stop sightseeing. That night, I fell asleep instantly. No more jet lag!

Day 8: Vienna

Last night was a great one! It was exactly what I needed. I woke up at 6:30AM and had breakfast in my room. Yesterday's muffin was delicious! The hotel also provided instant coffee and cream.

I decided to visit the flea market in the early morning. In the morning light, the opera house was stunning! The train station was nearly deserted because it was still early.

Line 4 was just one stop from the market, right outside the train station.

A keyboard piano was the first thing I saw at the market. There were approximately 150 stalls. Although it was only 8 AM, the market was already crowded with people, most of them locals. A stall sold me an old key with wings and I paid 2 euros. I was curious about the door that this key opened. Then, I purchased a ring at another stall for 15 euro.

Later, I joined the ladies to look through a pile of clothes and enjoyed a great time with them. I finally purchased a shirt and a sports coat. The jacket was essential because it was so cold!

After the market, I was too tired to return to my hotel so I decided to visit Albertina for the free tour. I was greeted by a huge pink rabbit as I passed the opera house on my way! There were actually many rabbits all around! Later, the tour guide revealed that Albertina had a tiny drawing of a rabbit as one of its greatest works. This is why all the colourful rabbits were placed in the city's centre. How adorable! About 200 people waited to be taken on the tour. They split us into two groups. Wolfgang was a middle-aged man who has a dry sense for humour.

First, we went up to Albertina. It was a beautiful view from the top. However, the sad tale of the opera house was not good. Wolfgang shared the sad story of the two architects who committed suicide soon after the opera house was completed because it didn't appeal to the Emperor. A monorail runs through the square near Albertina.

The Jewish victims. There were too many of us, and sometimes I couldn't hear Wolfgang!

The next stop was Hofburg. King Joseph was a king who had compassion. He was a king of compassion, protected the poor and fought against the Catholic churches. He had some unusual policies when he was older. For example, only comedies were allowed in theatres to avoid telling more tragic stories. To stop people spending too much money on extravagant funerals, he encouraged mass burials. Mozart was therefore buried in a large grave, not because he had died poor. It was enormous. It was used as a winter palace. We could rent one of the 400 rooms. However, the tour did not take us inside any of these buildings.

We had lunch at a cafeteria after our tour. On the tour, I met an Indian man. His wife was Taiwanese, and they lived together in Saudi Arab. For the English exams, he worked at Cambridge University. They had a daughter, and they were planning to move to Taiwan very soon. They bought a house in Tainan, his wife's hometown. The amazing beef soup that I had at the cafeteria was only 5 euros. After our break, we walked towards the shopping district, passing the oldest cafe of Vienna.

Wolfgang claims that Mozart lived in a small building right next to ours. This is what you can imagine! Wolfgang also mentioned Figlmuller, whose schnitzel was among the best in town. I was tempted to return to the kitchen to give it another try!

The impressive S. Stephen's Cathedral was located at the end the Kaerntnerstrasse. People were everywhere in the famous shopping street. Due to my dance lesson, I had to cancel the tour. I gave Wolfgang 10 euros as TripAdvisor reviews suggested. He was kind enough to tell me the location of the dance school and the tram route to the central cemetery. I said good-bye to the Indian man.

Vienna was one of my favorite cities. The historic buildings were beautiful and well-maintained unlike Havana's decayed glory. Vienna was very different from other Italian cities. It was more clean and orderly!
I had to return to the hotel to get my dancing shoes so I was late for my waltz lesson. Peter was a young instructor. He was tall and polite, wearing a suit. Although he knew I was not a beginner, he began with the basics. He didn't want me to learn the reverse step, as it was more difficult. After I asked him, he showed me the reverse step, but it was too late to practice.

Although he claimed that it took 50 minutes, the lesson was only 40 minutes long. Although I was late, I paid 62 euro for the lesson. It would have been nice if they had made an allowance for me. Although he said that he had another class for me, I didn't see any waiting when I left. Although the dance school was one among the most well-known and oldest in Vienna, I found it disappointing!

After the lesson, we went to Figlmuller for lunch. Most people were told by the waiter that the restaurant was full and suggested they go to the branch just around the corner. I heard him tell the couple in front of us so I went to the branch. The line was long, so I went back to the main restaurant. I was ushered inside by the waiter. Ha!! Ha! I was proud to have eaten about a third of the schnitzel. It was torture to feel like you had to eat it all, so I stopped, even though it was perfect!

I then went into the cathedral to take a look. It was beautiful and peaceful inside. The majority of Austrians are Catholic. The number of people shopping on the street was increasing. Swarovski was the most well-known Austrian brand after Porsche, so I had to go check it out! I purchased a beautiful ring for just 89 Euros!

After returning to my hotel, I took a rest before heading out for the concert. After a short nap, I went to the concert hall. As I was walking to the concert hall, I came across a young man selling tickets. I told him I was already booking a concert tonight, and he asked me if I wanted to purchase a ticket. It's something I regret to this day. I didn't say "yeah, what's your problem?" All of those touts wore historical costumes.

Some were extremely aggressive.

I tried to get a ticket for tomorrow's open-day opera house, but the ticket office was closed. I met another tout when I ventured outside. He was polite, well-spoken, and courteous. He was polite and well-spoken after I explained what I was looking for. Although I knew it was free, I was still very happy with the result. He was definitely more sophisticated than the first guy.

With the help of GPS, I found Musikverein... An older couple from Japan was also waiting outside. I asked them to take a picture of me in Japanese. They were surprised. It was breathtaking! I arrived half an hour before the closing time so I had a decaf and a chocolate strawberry from the cafe downstairs. Every year, the New Year's Ball takes place in The Gold Hall. It's easy to imagine elegant people dancing, laughing and having a great time!

It was amazing! The usher did not give me the correct instructions so I ended up in the wrong row. It said Row 1, Seat 6, but I chose Row I, Seat 6. This was the first row, and I couldn't see the stage. The most expensive ticket was 105 euros, so I was disappointed. One of my Chinese friends was sitting next to me and asked me about the seat. The usher was there and he showed me the correct seat. The rows I, II, and III were the first three rows. My row is the next. Row 1. Row 1!

The warning about no photos was made before the concert began in several languages, including Japanese, Chinese, and Japanese. However, the Chinese woman in my previous seat was taking pictures... during intermission I reminded her that the concert hall personnel could tell her off. She thanked me for my help and promised not to do it again. She didn't do it again, as someone else did it later. We were instantly told off! A woman complimented me on my beautiful dress while I was at the ladies!

The first piece they played was Mozart, but the final one was The Blue Danube. This is the second national anthem in Austria. It was amazing to hear that familiar tune performed by the Austrian Orchestra at the magnificent concert hall, where the New Year Ball takes place every year. I was close to tears! When I returned to the hotel, it was almost midnight. I was exhausted, but I went to sleep that night feeling elated!

Day 9: Vienna

Around 6:30am, I woke up with a cough. My cough was worsening. After having breakfast in my bedroom, I went to the central cemetery via tram at 9 a.m. Here, dogs were allowed anywhere except on the tram. The tram stopped after 30 minutes and everyone got off. I was told by a black man to get off because it was the last stop. He then gestured for me to follow him to the tram that was still waiting. I thanked him for his help and followed the instructions. After 1 stop, I was a little late and got off at an incorrect stop. There were many gates in the huge cemetery. Gate 2 was the gate I needed, but I ended up getting gate 1. There was a flower shop nearby so I bought 5 white roses for 2 euros each!

Then, I was lost. As I walked among the dead, it felt strange to be the only one breathing there. It was also very quiet. It was also a strange place for birds. Finally, I discovered civilisation again. I used the loo in the church. Then, I found 32A in the cemetery. Phew!! !

Many famous people lived here. I was so emotional... It was unbelievable that I made it! There were so many reasons to not go. It was pouring. It was only 40 minutes to the cemetery and I was running out time.

I still had to go to 2 palaces, 1 museum, and an opera house open house that day. But I couldn't resist! I had to stop by and say thanks for all their amazing music and the joy they have brought me over the years. There were also some Austrian tourists. I was asked by the man who took my picture if I was a musician. I answered that I did not play professionally, but I did play. Some of them smiled at my face.

Next, I rode the tram back to Belvedere and got off at a beautiful palace. It was now a gallery. Klimt was why I went there. I stayed only for half an hour and then took Tram D back to the city. I had lunch at the restaurant next to my hotel. The covered terrace was popular with people. They were kept warm by the heaters. It was delicious! I had roast pork with sauerkraut, white bread dumplings and white bread. Yum! My hotel was right across the street. The hotel wifi was even available! !

After a quick rest in the hotel, it was time to head out on Line 4 to the Schonbrunn summer palace, which is only 5 stops from my stop. After I entered, the staff told me to return to the ticket office with my Vienna card. I found the ticket office and went outside. I presented my card to the man and was instructed to enter the garden. I tried to go in, but I couldn't find the way into the palace. I returned outside and asked him again. I was finally given a ticket. I accepted the ticket and entered the palace. I was then told to wait 15 minutes. This was the time I was allocated to .....

After much fuss, I finally got in at 4pm. I was too busy to listen to the audio guide so I just walked through each room quickly. Before I saw the no photos sign, I snapped a picture of a ceiling. Oooops!

I then went to the large garden at the back. I bought a rose petal from the back and decided to keep it as my souvenir. These were Cici's roses. I powered walked back to the station later. A couple was taking their wedding photos at the exit. I snapped a photo of the yellow roses in bloom as I was walking to the station. They smelled like lemons!

Karlsplatz was my usual stop. However, I took the wrong exit, and I found a beautiful park. Sometimes getting lost has its advantages! I used GPS to get back to my hotel, but it led me to a beautiful cafe.

I was reminded that I had to make sachertorte. Wikipedia says:

Sachertorte refers to a particular type of chocolate cake or torte that was invented by

Austrian Franz Sacher in 1832 for Prince Wenzel von Metternich in Vienna,

Austria. It is one the most well-known Viennese culinary delights. December

National Sachertorte Day is celebrated on 5th of every month in the United States.

I was impressed by the cafe's classiness and charm, so I went in. I ordered decaf coffee. The cake and coffee were both delicious! The waiters were rude however! Three Taiwanese women came in and requested to share my table with me. Naturally, I agreed. They were on a tour. They were a beautiful cafe with delicious cakes and coffee, but I won't be back!

Then, I went to House of Music. First, I was amazed to see a man playing the grand-piano in the lobby. A teenage boy was next and he was also brilliant! Many people, mostly children, waited in line to play the grand piano. There were many young musicians playing the grand piano. It was getting late so I began exploring the museum. A piano keyboard was the first flight of museum stairs. It's so cute!

The museum had a section for all the composers. Hello Beethoven! We would love to see you again! Many people, mostly children and teenagers, are waiting patiently in another room as they wait for a virtual conductor to be called.

Vienna Philharmoniker. It was a course I wanted to try! The Blue Danube proved to be too difficult to conduct so I attempted a march instead. It worked out well! Ha! The Austrians clearly want to make classical music more accessible, relevant and contemporary. One floor is dedicated entirely to electronic and digital music. One of the floors hosts a young composer's work. It is a mix of Beethoven and Mozart, with a touch of house and techno. A couple of young parents and their babies were enjoying a Sunday afternoon together in the museum. It's no wonder Vienna is known as the music capital of Europe. It is best to get them started young. When I was three years old, I took my first piano lesson!

Then, I returned to the hotel to take a break. I took a power nap and then started to clean out my purse. I saw my opera open home tickets and realized that I was already half an hours late. It was just across the street, so I raced to get to the opera house.

After entering the opera house, my first stop was to check out the box seats. It was like there was a huge party going on! Then, I discovered the wardrobe department. There were many people playing, both children and adults. You could also see them getting their faces painted. The entire wardrobe department became a playground for all ages. They laughed as they tried on different opera costumes and were then made up by professional makeup artists. Then, they had their photos taken.

It was heaven! Do I look like a lady now? My new shirt's sleeves even matched my dress! It was so much fun!

Next, I went to the backstage. It was a large playground for both children and adults. It was amazing to see how big the backstage could be! NZ Opera is small compared to this! Many were dressed in costumes. Children loved the dry ice machine and the gold paper dispenser, but some preferred bubble glitter. The festivity is just amazing! The backstage was also home to props and sound/light equipment, which were explained and displayed.

We were able to roam around free-ranging. The majority of the areas were accessible. The choir rehearsal room was open to our inspection. The practice room had a grand piano and La Traviata music on some tables. Opened dressing rooms were available for the lead actor and actress.

Unfortunately, I was unable to attend the recital in the ballet room. Then, I heard "Peter"

So I was intrigued to find out more about Wolf1 and discovered a mini-concert! It was beautiful! It was so beautiful that I nearly started to dance to the music. Okay, I did wiggle a little... I continued my exploration after the mini concert. I snapped a photo of the beautiful corridor. A young man walked past and asked me if I would like a picture taken. I declined. He then asked me if I would like to take a picture with him. Boys will always be boys!

The evening concluded with a spectacular concert. The performance started at 7:30pm. It featured several opera teasers and a ballet teaser. There was also a stunning demonstration of visual effects like fireworks, dry ice, lights and fireworks. A video of a rollercoaster was shown to show sound effects. Also, there was a comedy dance that showed the speed of changing clothes. Finally, there were discussions about stage design and set changes. The fascinating concert covered all aspects of operas. Six languages were displayed on each screen.

The Vienna State Opera made operas more fun tonight! Operas are essentially singing and playing. Operas should be fun! Tonight

I was impressed by the efforts they made to include the public. It was held to celebrate the start of the new opera season, which would begin the next day. It would also be a great opportunity to produce young opera lovers for the future.

The only tickets for tomorrow's Turandot were gone, so I gave up on this trip. I returned to my hotel room at 9pm, and then updated my journal.

What a day!

Day 10: Budapest

I had a great night's sleep and woke up feeling refreshed this morning. After a quick breakfast, I started packing. With all my souvenirs, it was getting harder to pack everything in my one suitcase. I took Line 1 and arrived at the main station two stops later. I arrived almost an hour before the time. Although it was a large station, the signs were clearly posted. It was a long wait at the platform. While I waited, I saw a train leaving the station. I initially thought that someone was playing an oboe, but then I realized the train's engine was actually playing the scale. It was amazing! It's unbelievable .... Vienna even has trains that are musical?

Although I was only in Vienna for 3 days, I could clearly see how operas and classical music are an integral part of Austrian life. They are not only for the wealthy. This is how their musical heritage is passed down from generation to generation. This is also why their passion for music will never cease. This is not only true in Vienna. The two leading singers of La Traviata in Rome were simply amazing! They would have been considered national treasures if they were born in NZ. But, in Rome they were just singing to tourists. The truth is that the best singers and musicians from NZ all travel to Europe, and the best stay in Europe. NZ cannot afford to have the best. They don't have a market. I've been twice to NZ Opera open days. But I cannot say I was impressed.

At home, I am often puzzled why 90% of people who attend Auckland Philharmonia Orchestra concerts or NZ Operas are older than 65. The musicians, mostly Asians, would make up the majority of those under 30. What is the story? What are the Kiwis doing? What is it like to watch All Blacks? Tramping and hiking? What about properties? Sailing? APO Crescendo member. I support Connect. This program sends APO musicians out to teach children in low-decile schools, and gives free concerts.

But is this enough? What is the government doing? It is sad to think that classical music will soon die in NZ after our generation has gone. To whom will these young Asian musicians then play? They will be playing to each other?

Perhaps I should move to Vienna. Then, I might start learning German!

So I asked an American couple to help me find a number for my ticket. I was able to find a girl with a ticket that didn't have numbers so I let them know. I finally found a seat in the first class carriage, which I thought it was, and sat down. It was very comfortable. The waitress asked me what I wanted to drink, so I ordered a cappuccino. Two young policemen arrived and joined me in my room. I joked with them and said that I felt safer now that they were here. One of them smiled and said that this was why they were there. The ticket guy arrived about 15 minutes later and checked our tickets. He informed me immediately that I was in business class and not first class. I was offered 15 euro to upgrade, but I declined. I moved to the next carriage which was quite good. I didn't share a box! The cappuccino that I ordered was suddenly 2.9 euros so I declined. I instead had my last Mozart chocolate, and the water that I brought. It was enough for me. The coffee was not what I wanted anyway. I was able to update my journal because of the excellent wifi available in the train.

We stopped in Hegyeshalom, a Hungarian border town, about 50 minutes after we left Vienna. It was warm and sunny! Many cute train stations were found along the route. The train ride took 2 hours and 40 mins. The Budapest Central Station was impressive. I spent 20 euros at the station and then walked to the nearby subway station via the plaza. I purchased a 3-day pass at the station. Later, I followed the planned route to find my hotel.

The old-world charm of their subway stations was evident! The stunning opera house was the first thing I saw from the subway station. It was also right next to my hotel! The majority of hotels I booked were within walking distance to the state opera houses.

Since my GPS was out of commission, I used my map to navigate and it didn't make sense. Surprise surprise! Surprise surprise! I found the hotel! It was beautiful, 4-storey building with a lovely courtyard.

A sauna was also available for free. My key card opened 2 rooms, then I needed to use it again to enter my room in Room 102. The room was clean and there was chocolate on the pillows. It was very comfortable to sit on the sofa and dining table. The kitchenette was even included! It was too bad that there wasn't a bath. Another thing that I did not like was the lack privacy. It faced another building on busy streets, even though it was quiet. After I checked in, it was almost 1pm. I was hungry so I went hunting for food.

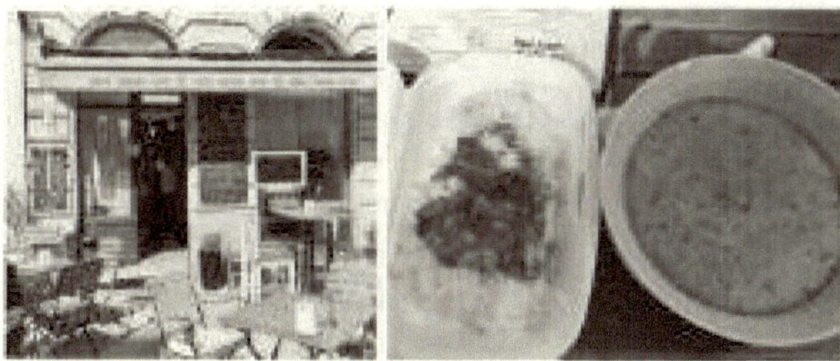

I couldn't find the restaurant recommended by my hotel so I went with the most popular one! I asked young girls for their recommendations and they recommended the traditional sausage and mushroom soup, with chicken. Yum! On the way back, I stopped at a cheese shop to buy a bottle sparkling water. There were so many wonderful shops around the area. A restaurant that offered a Thai-Japanese combo was located in my neighborhood. Hmmmm.

After taking a short nap, I decided that it was time to relax and take a break from the sightseeing. I just sat in my room. I got up at 7pm and set out to find the location of the musical I had reserved. I had to change trains twice. Derek Square was the first change. There was also a market. It was obvious that I needed to see it!

The street food was something that I was interested in. The food looked very appealing to me, but I wasn't able to buy anything!

I continued my subway ride to the opera. It was so much fun to look at the stations in their subways! Budapest is home to the oldest European subway.

I was greeted by a couple in good clothes at the last stop. I presented my ticket to them and they enthusiastically nodded. They directed me in the right direction. When I got inside, I was greeted by a Japanese woman wearing kimono. Subalashi, which means "wonderful" in Japanese, was what I told her. She smiled at me and thanked me for it!

All the performances were moved to other theatres while the opera house was being renovated. Erkel was a member of the state opera group. I found the musical "Csodaszarvas" quite fascinating, even though I couldn't speak Hungarian. Since all operas were in languages other than my own, I assumed I had sufficient training. But, one thing I didn't realize was that operas were stories I knew before the musical. This was a major difference from the musical. I was able to recognize some characters as angry and a servant trying to kill the prince.

I was pleasantly surprised when the man sitting next to me began talking to me during intermission. He was there with his wife, and his son. He was with his son, who was visiting them from

Melbourne! They were patient with me and explained the story. This musical was about Hungary's origins! I was in the middle of the first row. Talk about front and center! I was so close to stage, I could see the sweat on the faces of the male dancers. Those lads must have been very fit. Despite not being able to understand the language, I was able to enjoy the dance and music. The Hungarian folk dance, especially the footwork of male dancers, was amazing. It was a difficult dance. It reminded me a lot of Irish dance, which is another difficult folk dance.

To be completely honest, I was almost unable to go tonight due to feeling tired.

But, I am glad I did. It was worth it for the folk dance alone. I was able to reverse the train ride and find my way back easily. I was worried because there wasn't anyone on the street. It wasn't even 10:30pm. Evidently, the locals didn't stay up too late. The train was empty of passengers. I returned to the hotel and enjoyed some snacks and sangria, before retiring to my room for the night.

Day 11: Budapest

Around 5am, I was awakened by the street noise outside. However, I managed to get back to sleep for an hour. It was okay. Even though there was a variety of cooked foods, my favorite was the berry yogurt. It tasted amazing! My city tour began at 9:40 AM. I asked a street person for directions as the front desk was crowded with people trying to check out. I was already aware that the office of the tour company was close to my hotel. He was kind and helpful though. He later used Google Map to show me the way.

It was right by the opera house! We started after waiting for 15 minutes. Segway tours were also offered by them. That is something I should try! George, our guide, said that this area of the opera house was featured in the movie "Spy." There was a person who died there. You should go back to the movie! This street is where Tom Hank was kidnapped in Inferno. George, the guide, was in his twenties. He was very friendly.

Our first stop was Heroes Square. Naturally, I wanted to ask George why there weren't any heroines. He said that Cici had been there before, but they had moved her. We crossed a beautiful bridge. The artificial lake was beautiful.

It was located next to a beautiful building and looked very convincing!

George says that this castle was built from cardboard boxes in the beginning. It began to heat up. The lawn was filled with sunbathers. We passed the largest bathhouse in Budapest. I'd definitely return tomorrow!

The tour was attended by 12 people. Because I had purchased the 3-day pass the previous day, I wasn't required to purchase a train ticket. Next was the cathedral. However, we didn't go inside.

George instead led us to a strudel home. It was absolutely delicious when we entered! It was about noon, so I was hungry.

I chose cherry and poppy seed flavours. Yum! George later told us to take a look at our toilets so we went for a scenic trip to the ladies. Wow! It was truly stunning!

After our break, we walked by a statue. George said that rubbing the stomach of this man will bring you good luck. We then made our way across the Chain Bridge to the Buda side. The Buda side was quite hilly. It was like a fairytale castle! We reached the top to find a magnificent cathedral. There was a large crowd outside at the plaza. David and Danielle were both from South Africa. They spent two months each year at their Parnell, NZ house. Later, we exchanged email addresses.

We went inside the cathedral after the tour. I was impressed! George recommended that I use the stairs to descend the hill. With all the flowers in bloom, it was beautiful.

The River Danube was nearly as large as the ocean! George advised me to take bus 105 back to the hotel.

It was almost 2:30 pm when I got back. I was hungry so I went back to the same cafe for lunch. It was delicious! It was delicious! The cream chicken rice and chicken soup were amazing! I returned to the hotel later and received a free glass of lemonade.

A little note was left on my bed in my bedroom.

"The phrase of the Day from Hotel xxxxxx: When someone really wants something, the universe conspires with him to realize his dream. (Paulo Coelho). Your room was cleaned and vacated by xxxxxx. Date xxxxx'

Nice touch! The same housekeeper returned later, when I was calling another tour company to confirm tonight's tour. I was also changing clothes, so I was still half naked! She kept knocking at the door, so I went to the front door and asked her to return later. She spoke something that I couldn't understand so I told her I wouldn't need any housekeeping. She finally left after grumbling something. After I had called her, I called the front desk to complain.

Tonight was the River Danube sunset cruise. Around 6:15 pm, a driver picked me up. We stopped at a nearby hotel to pick up a couple on our way. There were many people on the boat, all excited! Everyone was busy taking pictures! After I asked a Thai girl for a photo of me, she asked her friend to do one of us together. Eugene may have been right. I felt like an UNESCO site. People wanted photos with/of me!

It was breathtaking to see the sunset over the Danube. The parliament is third in size worldwide. George, the guide suggested we go take a look. If I have the time tomorrow, I might! The majestic building was lit up as it was getting dark!

The Chain Bridge was also lit up! With all the lights on, the beautiful city was transformed into a magical land. Buda Castle was breathtaking! The young people hooted as we passed another bridge. They stayed on top deck, despite it raining!

Although my iPhone could not capture the amazing view, I tried! During the 2-hour cruise, I took around 300 photos. Most of the photos had to be deleted later. Budapest shone in the darkness. It was simply stunning!

I'm so happy that I took the cruise trip! Every 5 minutes, the gallery's colours changed. Most fascinating! It was cold and I felt it on the deck, even though it was covered. I decided to go downstairs to the dinner buffet. I decided not to eat the buffet because I did not want to eat too much at dinner. The main hall was also lit up! Josoin, a solo traveller from Holland, was also present. We talked all night and then exchanged email addresses. By the time I get home, I'll have made a lot of new friends. First, I tried champagne. Then I decided to try strawberry juice. We went upstairs to take more photos as the boat got closer to the dock. I thought the Chain Bridge looked even better at night! Someone spotted my red wristband near the exit and accompanied me to the driver when I got off the boat. Around 9:30pm, I was dropped at my hotel. It was a great way to end an amazing evening!

Then, I set out to find the central marketplace. The escalators at their subway stations move at lightning speed. It's very frightening! !

It was huge at the central market! For lunch, I bought a cabbage roll. It was quite good! Many souvenir shops upstairs sold beautiful laces. George, our guide, told us yesterday that there were many pickpockets in the area.

At a popular bakery, I bought some freshly-out-of-the-oven mini cabbage buns and ate them while walking around. I also purchased a cherry pie to make tomorrow's breakfast. The sausage shops were the most popular shop in the market!

An exquisite lace coaster was purchased for 5 euros later. I walked back to the subway station and found a pharmacy so I bought plasters for my blister. The tram was adorable! The high-end shopping district was where the opera house was. Some singers were still practicing outside the opera house. They were amazing. They worked hard under the bright sun. I bought the ticket for the 4pm tour at the opera house.

Budapest was so much more beautiful than I had expected. It was tiny but beautiful! I returned to my hotel and took an apple from the hallway table, and brought it into my room. They really made an effort! After a short nap, I took the photos and edited them in my journal. During my stay, the 72 hour travel card was very helpful. I was ready to go for the tour of the opera house at 3:50 p.m. It was quite fascinating to see the building behind the hotel.

Near the hotel was a gym. A few people shouted at the nearby cafe. Opera rehearsals were still going on.

The English group in the opera house was so large that they had to divide us into two. Although there weren't many Japanese tourists, I felt more at home using English. Five languages were available. The auditorium floor was actually an audioboard. The opera house was currently under renovation. The next opera will be in 2019!

The royal box was reserved only for three people: the president of Hungary and the primary minister. It was used only once by King Frances Joseph. It is a complete waste. According to the guide, the side boxes were the most expensive in the house. One cost 80 euros, which is about half the price of other opera houses. Cici's box was our destination. Although she could only see half the stage from her box, she chose it as everyone could see her... Talking about narcissists!

According to the guide, there were actually some people who stayed at the bar while the opera was on because they wanted to socialize! Secret rendezvous were also possible in the smoking room. People couldn't see one another because of the thick smoke. The public had a wonderful staircase, but the staircase leading to the royal box was breathtaking for the royalty. The mirror was meant to be a helper in admiring the room. Cici loved the mirror, but she probably used it to admire her own room!

It was breathtaking to see the view from the royal boxes. Later, I felt very royal sitting in the royal box. This opera house was the first to have an iron curtain. The English was very fluent in our guide. We were able to enjoy a five-minute mini-concert after the tour. The opera cafe was amazing!

The staff was busy setting up the stage outside the opera house. It's too bad that I won't be able to attend tomorrow's show. I walked into a beautiful clothes shop, but the sizes were too large. I next went to a butchery where I bought a sausage. To see why sausages are so popular in the area, I had to taste some. I discovered a cafe with kindergarten-style tables and chairs. I was ready to be a child so I ordered the beef soup. I was given a lemonade free of charge for my long wait. It was delicious. I gave them five euros and all my Hungarian coins. They wouldn't accept credit cards.

When I got back to the hotel, the package was opened from the butchery. Inside was a large sausage! The mustard was generously provided by them! Although I struggled to finish the sausage, it became the second course of my meal. Although it was my last evening in the beautiful city, I was still recovering from all of the walking and sightseeing so I decided to stay in for a quiet night. I also had to be up at 5am the next morning. I would be picked up by a taxi at 7am to take me to the airport!

Day 13: Prague

I woke up at 5am to have breakfast in my bedroom. Yesterday's cherry pie from Central Market was delicious! I was picked up by a taxi driver around 7:15 AM. He was a nice young man who spoke good English. We chatted quite a bit. We arrived at the airport about 30 minutes later. They told me to bring cash, but the driver didn't have any euros so I paid 20 instead. This airport had a very strict security screening. For explosives checks, they asked me to open my suitcase and shoulder bag. The suitcase was too heavy for me, but my shoulder bag was fine. I wanted to tell them that I would open the suitcase, but I needed to ask them to please close it. I was the mother of the baby. They also checked the milk and baby food! They were doing their job, but I took it seriously. What about baby food? The gate number was not available for me until almost an hour later.

1.5 hours later, I was in Prague. Many drivers were outside, holding signs with different names for their guests. To find my driver, I had to go around twice! To get to my hotel, it took us around 20 minutes. My room was not ready, so I asked the staff for suggestions on lunch and then set off to explore. Beautiful arches were found in the building across the street. A man tied a dog to a lamppost at the corner of the church. The poor dog was aware that it would be left outside, waiting. Old Town Square was magnificent! I found the restaurant using my GPS. I ordered beef neck and steamed. Both were delicious! They made their own beer. Their beer tank was very nice!

The old church was still visible from my square. Along with hundreds of tourists, I watched the 1:05 o'clock program from the clock tower. Near the hotel were beautiful pink flowers!

The hotel was beautiful. The lobby was historic. They were still there when I returned.

Finally, I had my room. Room 418 was the attic room, and it was located at the end on the hallway at the top floor. A full-length mirror was found in the room.

Although the bathroom was basic, it was functional.

After a quick nap, I was ready to go and meet Robert, my architectural tour guide, in front of The Powder Tower. St James Cathedral was our first stop. It was a Gothic building with a baroque façade. Robert says that the baroque style was created to restore faith in God. Gothic cathedrals had three doors, but they converted to the baroque style. The two side doors would be sealed, while the interior arches would remain typical gothic. The beautiful art nouveau Municipal House was our second stop. This was now a concert venue. It was beautiful! It was a great place to see a concert. Robert gave me his Indian scarf to keep me warm because it was so cold. He was very kind! The bridge connected the Municipal House to the chapel at Powder Tower.

Power Tower was our third stop. It was a beautiful baroque building. Next, we visited a Cubist building. Now it was a museum. It was quite impressive! On our way to the Luxemburg king's compound, we passed this adorable witch. The compound also contained a brothel. The sign had seven candles that indicated the brothel was open 7 days per week!

We then went to a cafeteria in an old Renaissance building.

Robert says that Renaissance was inspired in part by Roman architecture. I ordered a decaf coffee and a honey cake. Yum! Robert had a beer and an espresso, as well as a cheese. Both of us were charged the same price. It cost only 10 euros. It was so out of tune!

Robert was half Nigerian and half Czech. He was half-Czech and half-Nigerian. He also had a master's in tax accounting. After our break, we checked out the Roman building next to us. Were Romans short like me?! The Tyn Cathedral was stunning in its gothic splendor. A beautiful baroque building was also visible as we walked by it. We finally reached the Jewish Quarter. All the top brands were found here. These buildings looked like castles and were all neo-renaissance. One was built by a wealthy Jew and used as his Facebook wall. The facade's symbols were all for selfpromotion. Robert thanked me and I walked back to square. It was about 6 p.m.

I was given a complimentary beer from the hotel's restaurant/bar. It was delicious, but I wasn't ready to drink alone so I took the beer from the hotel bar and drank it in my room. I also had almonds and pistachio nuts. Although it was a long day, it was an excellent start to my stay in Prague!

Day 14: Prague

I slept for almost 10 hours! That was a good thing! It was quite a feast. The breakfast included not only cold food, but also hot food such as eggs, bacon, and fried vegetables. Even a bottle chilled champagne was available! The porridge was excellent! It was also a delight to have breakfast in the morning. The hotel was located in a beautiful historical building.

After eating a big breakfast, I went to the shower and set off for another day of adventure. The locals love classic cars, but they were actually available for hire. It reminded me of Havana!

The famous Charles Bridge was then found. It was just after nine o'clock in the morning, so there were not many people or stalls around. The new town was on the other side of river. After climbing up the hill for 10 minutes, it took me nearly 20 minutes to reach the castle compound.

There was a long line. There were soldiers guarding the old palace. A brass band was seen passing by. The cathedral was just as fascinating. Amazing stained glass windows! The old royal palace was next. I was glad I didn't listen to Robert, the guide's suggestion to skip the palace. It was stunning!

It was breathtaking from the palace. I also visited St George Cathedral. There were many cute shops along the Golden Lane. I nearly bought a pink bell, and a little dish in blue.

It was also lovely to see the wreath on the front door. I bought only two small magnets and decided to be sensible. There was also an address for a psychic.

Then, I saw an unusual statue! Finally, I wandered into Lobkowicz Palace. My ticket didn't cover this palace museum, and I was too tired.

I left.

It was a long climb. There was a juice stand at the bottom of the hill. I nearly bought a juice, but decided to resist. I followed the sign to the metro station. The ticket booth at the station was not where they sold tickets. I bought my ticket at this convenience store located near the booth.

These escalators were more friendly than the ones in Budapest. They were slower! It was quite cool to see the station design! Although their trains were quite old, they were well-designed. It took me one stop to get to my hotel.

Only a block from the station was Rudolfinum, a grand concert hall. Although there was a bridge right next to the concert hall, I was too tired and couldn't walk. On the way to lunch I stopped at a shop where I bought a pair crystal earrings for 25 euros. Lokal was my lunch place. I had pork knuckle soup and cucumber salad this time. Delish!! They eat pork knuckle, too! They are good people! !

On my return to the hotel after lunch, a man claiming to be a lawyer tried to introduce me. He was going to Australia in two weeks.

Prague!
Bahahahahahahahahahahahahahahahahahahahahahahahahahahahahahahahaha
hahahahahahahahahahahahahahahahahahahahahahahahahahahahahahahaha
hahahahahahahahahahahahahahahahahahahahahahahahahahahahahahahaha
hahahahahahahahahahahahahahahahahahahahahahahahahahahahahahahaha
hahahahahahahahahahahahahahahahahahahahahahahahahahahahahahahaha
hahahahahahahahahahahahahahahahahahahahahahahahahahahahahahahaha
hahahahahahahahahahahahahahahahahahahahahahahahahahahahahahahaha
hahahahahahahaha I was tired by the time I got back to the hotel. I took a break and decided to take photos at Rudolfinum. High heels were killing me on cobblestone streets so I returned to my hotel to change. Then, I went for a walk. I had to try the famous ice cream pastry. These shops were all over the place! Robert stated that they appeared suddenly about 10 years ago, and that this Czech dessert is now a 'traditional1 Czech dessert. I tried one with vanilla ice-cream. Heaven! The street wall featured a beautiful painting

of a goddess. It was interesting to see what other tourists thought. Later, as I was walking past a church I noticed a sign advertising concerts. I was excited to see my favorite Czech piece, Smetana's Moldou, so I bought a ticket.

So I stopped by a street artist and asked him about his beautiful paintings. He preferred Budapest in the rain. I purchased 3 small prints from him. Each print cost only 3 euros! I also spoke to the artist's dog! He was a very cool guy! On the square in the old town, someone was playing with snakes, something he shouldn't have!

I then walked by a Thai massage shop and decided to take a look, as I had two hours before tonight's concert. For 55 Euro, I got a 30 minute back massage and 40 minute foot massage. The fish ate the dead skin of people's feet. Yuk! My masseuse

Tic was excellent so I gave her 5 euros (about 10%) as tip and booked her for the next day.

The next day, at 7:30pm. I was given a 20% discount card by her! As a single mother of an 18-year-old son, she had lived in Prague for four years. When I left the massage parlour, the sun was setting on the square. A young, brilliant pianist was playing Chopin. I returned to the hotel at 6:30pm, and took a break.

In my sandals, I walked to Rudolfinum. Outside, a band was playing when I arrived. Everyone was dressed up, except me, once I got inside. Oooops! It was incredible! The concert was nearly full house. The London Philharmonic Orchestra performed Shostakovich, Prokofiev, and Dvorak. Although it was an unusual program, and filled with emotions, I didn't enjoy the Shostakovich part. It was an understatement. It was too much!

Although the concert was over by 10:30, I stayed to interview Vladimir Jurowski. Although he was intelligent, he seemed a little arrogant. He was intelligent but a bit arrogant. However, I began to like him after he confessed that he was nervous tonight conducting Dvorak in the composer's concert hall!

The interview ended at 11:59 pm. It was freezing cold and I was shivering as I walked back to my hotel. But I was glad I was wearing sensible shoes! !

Day 15: Prague

It was my last day here in Prague. It was a wonderful place, but there were so many things I wanted to do. After a huge breakfast, I went to Perfumed Prague to check out the top-rated shop on TripAdvisor. Despite it being almost 11 o'clock in the morning, the shop was still closed.

Outside, I met two American women. They were scheduled for an appointment at 11 AM. It was hilarious to discover that they had just come from Berlin, my next stop and were now going to Budapest, my final stop. It was a reverse journey! We were greeted by the staff at 10:55 am. They were kind enough to let me in, even though I didn't have an appointment. We were served tea and macaroons, and then we participated in a scent contest. I was awarded the prize, which was a seaweed soap. They actually gave the soap to the two other girls. Funny thing is, both of them worked at Lush and were very knowledgeable about fragrance. I believe I was lucky! We had to then choose between three layers of scents. Bryce, Olga's partner, was also very helpful.

We had to go outside for a bit so our noses could heal. The water was served in a glass shaped like a lightbulb! Two hours later, I had made my first personal perfume. It was named Prague Rose. I went to the mall and picked up the soap and perfume at the hotel. Palladium was recommended by TripAdvisor. It seemed like everyone was there. The mall was packed on Saturday. I purchased some dresses and decided not to pack. I was hungry so I went to the food court and found a Prague restaurant. I ordered the Old Prague Plate. Mama Mia! They love meat! The duck was a little dry. Many people waited outside for the drifter event to begin. I decided to leave because I had a concert I wanted to see.

I returned my clothes to the hotel and then power walked to Mirror.

Church. I arrived at the church around 5:20 p.m. I was the first to arrive! They let

We will be there at 5:35 p.m. It was beautiful! Two mirrors were placed on either side of the altar. That is how the church got its name. It was my dream that I could listen to Moldau in Prague. After all, the piece was about their river Vltava. It was a great performance by the string quartet, an organ player and a soprano. This 65-minute concert was far more enjoyable than the last night's!

Because it was getting cold, I returned to the hotel to get my denim jacket. I then walked the short distance to the massage parlour. They told me that they had made a mistake in my booking and I would have to wait.

20 minutes. They offered to give me the fish for free, but I declined. I returned home and bought a bottle cherry cider. I drank it in my bedroom while my music was playing loudly. Yay!

Prague was a great city, but it's overrated. Budapest is my favorite city! Prague seems too touristy to me. !

Day 16: Berlin

After going to bed around 9pm last night, my neighbours woken me up at 10:30pm. They kept making louder and more annoying noises. I decided to give up sleep and watch the BBC until midnight. It was around 5:30 AM that I awoke this morning. My alarm was set for 6am so I decided to rise early.

After taking a shower, it was time to get breakfast. To snack on the train, I had an apple and an egg saved. It was amazing that I was able to zip up my suitcase. At 7:30 am, my taxi picked me up. It was pouring today. It was raining this morning.

Someone was playing the piano at the Prague train station. I waited patiently for the pianist to stop and then I started playing my song, "Autumn Is a Lady." There were many dogs at the station. I took many photos to entertain myself. I must get a pet dog!

I didn't know the number of my seat so I sat down until someone said to me to move. A ticket clerk arrived at the Prague station and advised me to change to the second class as I was in the first. The website I used to purchase the ticket was only available in Czech The website was in Czech, and I couldn't even see my ticket. Although I was allowed to upgrade, the ticket clerk informed me that the second class was only two carriages away. I decided to check it out so that I would be able to upgrade. This was probably a bad decision as I had to open heavy doors that read 'automatic' in English. The second class had a dining carriage that was very interesting! Finally, I found my way to the second class. I was already sweating even though it was just two carriages away, as the clerk said. To reward myself, I took a seat and ordered coffee. We passed many beautiful places along the banks of a river. It reminded me of Queenstown, NZ. It was close to the Czech/German border. It was near the Czech/German border. I promised myself that I would return one day!

It took approximately 5.5 hours to complete the journey. The grand central train station was my first impression of Germany - it was modern, beautiful, industrial, and spectacular! I purchased a 48-hour Berlin Welcome card and took the subway to MU Hotel, following the directions given me by the tourist center. Because there were different levels on each line, I lost my way in the subway station.

My journey to my hotel took almost an hour, despite the fact that it only took 15 minutes to travel by subway with one line change. With a suitcase, it was even more complicated. I'm going to order a taxi from the airport. My room, 518, was amazing! The room was spacious and sunny. But the best thing about it was the bathtub!

After a quick nap, I headed to the Riechstag. I was only about half an hour away from my hotel by train. It was 2 months ago that I made my admission reservations and it was a great decision. It was a packed house, with many people wanting to see the dome. The dome was amazing, but the view from the top was just as impressive!

Later, I walked to the subway to take pictures of the Berlin landmark. Many people were gathered in front of the gate. Funny thing was, I also saw policemen at the gate, as with all other tourist attractions in Europe.

I then took the subway to Berlin Philharmonic Concert Hall. The nearest station was approximately 10 minutes away. My sandals were again killing me... I passed the Sony Centre, which was the beautiful building that hosted the Berlin Film Festival every year. There were also concerts and premieres of movies. Although the world-famous Berlin Philharmonic Concert Hall doesn't look very impressive from outside, I felt goosebumps just thinking about the people who once performed there. I arrived 2 hours early. Many people arrived early to attend the pre-concert speech, but I did not because it was in German. As the hall filled up, I settled down for some drinks and sparkling water. It was amazing!

Tonight's conductor was Susanna Makki. This is a rare female maestro, especially when you consider the few female musicians in this orchestra, all of whom were wearing pants and their hair up high. Susanna Malkki was also there! It was hard to know what to make of it, but I felt that I was a feminist, but very feminine. Tonight, they performed Busoni's Tanz Walzer (my favorite tonight), Bartok's second violin concerto (the soloist Gil Shaham used his soul to play with his bow), as well as Sibelius' second symphony.

Two months ago, Michael Hill's violin competition at Auckland Town Hall was my first experience. I wrote this review shortly afterwards:

"Give me imperfection whenever!" Tonight's Michael Hill Violin Competition result has disappointed me deeply. The finalists are all extremely talented, and I can understand that it was difficult for the judges to choose the winners. However, passion is more important than perfection to me. Music is about passion! Passion!! Passion! I'm sorry the judges didn't agree with my vision.

Tonight's concert was a perfect example of passion and perfection. But what surprised me most was how they managed it together. It's not possible for a single musician to possess both the proper training and the right attitude, but it is almost impossible when there are over 100 musicians performing together. They did it, however, tonight under the direction of Susanna at the concert hall where Karajan laid down the foundation stone.

After the concert, I felt like I had been frozen for three hours. I could also feel a happy blister growing on my right foot. I took a taxi to get back to my hotel after the concert. There was a huge queue for taxis so I decided to walk instead. I finally got a taxi after walking for a block. Yay!! It cost only 10 Euros, including the tip. When I returned from the concert, I was still buzzing!

Berlin Philharmonic, another item on my bucket list! !

Day 17: Berlin

I woke up at 7:15 am, had a shower, and then went downstairs to have breakfast.

It was only 18 euros, but well worth it. It was amazing how many options there were! Naturally, I ate again! I also stole a banana, an egg and a peach. Today I went on a Berlin walking tour. I rushed to get there from my breakfast so I caught the train. Just as they were about to begin, I arrived just in time. Phew! I was interrupted by the guide and showed my reservation to her. She asked me if it was the right tour. The guide said that it was, but it was an English tour. Perhaps she hadn't seen an English-speaking Asian before!

We walked across the bridge first, before we started our tour. Beautiful cathedral was located by the river. The museum island was our first stop. This area contained 5 museums. Michael, our guide, encouraged us to go back later. It was a pity that I didn't have enough time or energy. Berlin seemed to have many museums! Michael pointed out a flat across the bridge and said that it was home to the German PM Angela.

We passed a building that was designed by Ieh Ming Pei (the architect who created the steel and glass pyramid at the Louvre).

Next, we visited a place where Nazis burned books. We also saw pink tubes, which were used to draw water from the swamp beneath Berlin.

We then went to see the famous Wall. The map showed the former East Germany and West Germany. I didn't realize Berlin was also divided.

two! Two walls made up the Berlin Wall: an inner and outer wall. They were separated by a death strip. Anyone who tried to cross the wall would have been shot.

The grey building that is behind the wall was home to the German secret police, which tortured and killed Jews. The East German government constructed many housing projects in the area of the Nazi old ground. This was where Hitler and his bride, who had just married, committed suicide.

The Jewish memorial was next. I was carrying my bag pack, which I had just purchased at a small mall during lunch. Michael, a British historian, had lived in Berlin for more than 18 years. His girlfriend was German, and he was still waiting to get his German citizenship. I asked him if he was experiencing a cultural identity crisis and he said that he considered himself to be German. It would be nice if things were that simple for me. Modern Germany is a product of a very dark past. Michael asked me how Germany's young people dealt with the guilt of their past. He stated that it was important for the country to remember its past. I suggested that American Jews living in Hollywood only reinforced the nation's guilt.

That was what the Germans were carrying. Then he told me something new about the Holocaust industry.

The gate was our last stop. The dome and Reichstag could be seen on our left. Although I had already paid online for the tour, I wanted to tip

Michael. But, I couldn't find any change, other than one 50-euro bill. So I gave up. After he finished, he invited everyone to join him for a drink. I would have loved to, but I was too tired. I had to change trains, but as I looked for the U2 station I noticed a sign for Sony Centre. I decided to go to the Sony Centre. I was looking for something Asian, so I went with sushi. Yum!! On my way, I stopped at the convenience store near the subway station to buy a beer! !

I returned to the hotel at 4pm. I requested that the hotel print my boarding pass, and then ordered a taxi to the airport. After editing today's photos, I updated my journal. Later, I watched old TV shows and had the beer along with the rest of my mixed nuts. I also ate the peach. It was delicious and very juicy. After that, I took a long soak and chilled out. It was a very thought-provoking day!

Day 18: Amsterdam

I was woken by the alarm at 6:01 AM I had been asleep for nine hours and only woke up once at 3am. I had a quick breakfast in my room. The coffee was excellent and I also enjoyed the banana and egg from the previous day. The hotel provided free apples for guests, so I grabbed one to snack on during my flight.

My taxi driver was punctual. The taxi cost only 25 euros and I tip him 2 euros. My perfume caused me to have to open my bag again at security. Next time, I will make a makeup bag. They provided us with delicious cakes and beverages during the 1 hour flight. The cake was delicious, I told the flight attendant. It looked like we were in a bubble bath under the clouds! As Amsterdam became visible, I saw many windmills. The first shop I saw was selling a strange-looking vegetable after landing. They were tulip bulbs, which I quickly realized. How Dutch are windmills and tulips!

I followed the signs directing me to the official taxi stand on the ground. However, it took me half an hour to find the taxi stand. After a 20-minute taxi ride I finally reached my hotel. Although the taxi cost me 40 euros, I was too tired to care. Although the staff at the hotel were very friendly, the room #4 they showed me was right next to the breakfast room. The children from the nearby kindergarten were screaming and playing outside the window. It was noisy, even though I requested a quieter room when I booked. They refused to upgrade me. The first room cost 130 euros per day, while the second was 160. Although it was better, the children's screams could still be heard.

After eating the apple, I took a short nap. After my nap, I felt much more energized and set off to explore the city. Although the hotel was nice from the outside I wouldn't stay there again. The playground was where the screaming children were playing. The window to my left, looking at the hotel from the play area, was the window that they had given me for my first room. It was no wonder that the room was so noisy. Then, I passed a magnificent concert hall. I went in to see the concert program, but nothing stood out.

My Van Gogh Museum reservation was for 2:30pm. I decided to make it in before that time. Sunflowers, a Van Gogh reproduction, was available to be smelt and touched. The museum was beautiful and modern. There was also a photo booth. The museum was well-designed to tell Vincent's tale. Vincent was such an artist who worked tirelessly, even though he became famous only because of his brother's support, and his sister-in law's continued efforts to promote his work after his death.

Next, I visited Rijksmuseum. Many people were milling about the quarter of the museum. The museum was located in an historic building. It was impressive. I knew the guy who sold me my ticket before he lived in Wellington. He advised me to go up the second floor, where Rembrandt used to be, and Night Watch. After visiting the museums, I took a tram to Dam Square where I could take my Red Light District tour. Many people were spotted in the square, as well as many pigeons. One boy was afraid of the aggressive pigeons and was crying. The cathedral on the right and the palace in the square were both spectacular.

I walked into an Indonesian restaurant after finding it. I was hungry! I ordered lamb biryani. Yum yum yum! Later, I walked by the canal. It was still there.

It was too early to go on the tour so I stopped by a cafe and ordered blackberry crumbs and herbal tea. Cocotte was the name of the cafe and their logo featured a rooster. I went upstairs to use the toilet, and took a picture from the stairs. It was a beautiful cafe!

After the break, my wallet was stolen from Zara. It had two credit cards and only 150 euros. Pickpockets pose a danger in every city. They are professionals and often work together in a group. Zara's security guard looked over the camera and found nothing. They suggested I report it to police and gave me the address of the station. I tried to locate it, but I failed. I returned to Zara to leave my name, my email address, and the name and hotel of my hotel so they could find my wallet. I then emailed my bank asking them to cancel the stolen cards.

Then, I took the Red Light District tour. Mark, our guide, was engaged in marriage to a prostitute working at the Red Light District. First, he took us to a condom store. We were seven of them. We huddled together in the cold wind, listening to Mark. All I wanted was to get back to my hotel. It was getting darker. I didn't have any money and no credit cards. I felt extremely vulnerable.

The tour was over. Mark helped me find a taxi that took credit cards. While I was back at my hotel, the driver waited outside and then returned to my room. He also took my other wallet. I used my bank debit card to pay the driver. Finally, I felt safe and warm in my bedroom.

Day 19: Amsterdam

I slept for 8 hours. Yesterday was exhausting! It was a huge spider that I first saw. I called the front desk to have the spider removed for me. He did it with his naked hands. Then, I went downstairs to have breakfast. This morning the internet was down. In fact, 2/3 of the country was affected by the storm! A lovely breakfast area was available at the hotel. They provided a delicious breakfast with freshly prepared eggs and crispy bacon. Even made crepes for us!

After breakfast, I went straight to the ATM to withdraw some cash. It was windy, but it wasn't raining. The lobby of the hotel was very cozy. You can also get a Night Watch from them!

I took the tram from Dam Square to Anne Frank House. My journey to Anne Frank House was made possible by the tram.

way, I saw a quirky shop selling rubber duckies! It was closed, so I decided to return later. Even in this weather, the canal was breathtaking.

While I was waiting to enter Ann Frank House, it started to rain heavily.

It was so windy, umbrellas were ineffective. I was able to keep my coat on! It was a flea market purchase that I made in Vienna, which was a blessing! I later discovered that many flights from Amsterdam were cancelled because of the storm!

The queue finally moved, just in the right time to avoid everyone getting soaking wet. After I was inside, I followed the crowd to a bookshelf. It was behind it that Anne had hidden for two years. It was an incredibly difficult experience. Many of the visitors left with tears in eyes. It was almost too real to believe that the number, the death toll of Jews, had suddenly become so large. How many Annes were murdered? What can we learn from history? Many historians say the answer is no. How will the world change? The following quote she wrote in her diary resonated with me: "When I write, all my worries disappear." My sorrow vanishes and my spirits are reborn. 5 April 1944 - I was glad I went.

I returned to the rubber duckie shop, but it was closed so I found a nearby cafe and had tea. The shop finally opened at 10:30 AM. I waited until then. It was almost like a museum of rubber duckies! My favorite was the bikini-clad duckie!

I then took the tram to Rembrandt House. I got off the tram, but couldn't choose which direction. When I was using my phone's map app, a man asked me if I needed any help. He was a young man working at the hotel. He was just finishing breakfast and was heading home. He was from that area! He was so kind! I was able to find my destination using his phone. We parted ways at the corner, and I continued on the path he had given me. I came across a cute shop selling flowers made of plastic. The area also had some colorful buildings.

Rembrandt purchased this mansion, and lived there for over 20 years. But in the end

He couldn't pay the mortgage so he sold it and went bankrupt. The kitchen was very warm and welcoming. The maid slept on a box bed in her kitchen. Rembrandt's bedroom was the next room. People used to sleep in a sitting position during their time because it was considered healthier. Beautiful was the living room. He did the etching work in a separate room. After waiting about 15 minutes, the demonstration began. It was very simple!

Rembrandt was an avid collector. Rembrandt collected almost everything. Rembrandt's paint mixing process was demonstrated by a woman. Finally, I was able to see his studio. His students occupied the top floor. Each cell was correctly divided. It was wonderful to visit Rembrandt House.

I purchased food from a nearby pharmacy and took a taxi to my hotel. I nearly walked into a nearby cafe, but I decided to stay in my safe room and eat the junk food that I bought earlier. I went back to my safe space and made instant noodles for lunch. Yay!! This was the most delicious meal I have had in my entire trip. After a short nap, I had some decaf coffee and a chocolate biscuit, then updated my journal. I watched half of the TV simultaneously. This was exactly what I needed! I felt normal again after taking a break from the sightseeing! After a shower, I packed my bag and went to bed. I'm hoping it will pass the airport inspection without being opened tomorrow!

Day 20: Madrid

I woke up at 5:45am, just before my 6 a.m. alarm. I had slept for almost 9 hours. It was exhausting to travel and I needed time to rest. I wasn't young anymore! After a quick breakfast, and a Nespresso in the lounge, I took a taxi with an elderly couple from South Africa to the airport. Although my suitcase was cleared by security, I had to open it to reveal all the small cream bottles. I also had the larger bottles in a zip-lock bag. I was happy to not have to open or close my suitcase. Even though I have done lots of traveling, I still feel nervous about travelling. I am slowly becoming insane from the nearby travelator's announcement that'mind your steps'. The sun finally appeared just as I was about to leave Amsterdam after two days of rain, storm and lightning. Hmmmmm... I arrived at the gate an hour before takeoff, and it looked almost deserted. I double-checked, and it was correct. It wasn't even here yet. Zzzzzzzzzz.

After half an hour, people began arriving. They were shouting and running in various languages. Children crying, businessmen barking into mobile phones, and children screaming. Amazingly, the plane flew on time. In KLM's magazine in-flight, I was able to read a Sir Paul Smith interview. It was very interesting, but I particularly liked the quote: "There's so many beauty in many small things such as laughter and eye contact, deep conversation, and even eye contact." This reminded me of the most delicious meal I've had so far on this trip, the instant noodles I made in my hotel room yesterday!

The black jacket was my favorite purchase on this trip.

The Vienna flea market. It was freezing in Vienna, Budapest Berlin, Berlin, and Amsterdam. The jacket is water-proof as well. Yesterday, as I was waiting at Ann Frank House to check in, the sky opened up and it started raining. It was so windy, umbrellas were ineffective. I was proud of my decision to purchase the jacket and not the pretty dress that I had been eyeing at the time. I was able to keep from getting soaked yesterday by the jacket.

Paul Smith's designs have always been a favorite of mine. The wallet that was stolen was actually a Paul Smith. It was quite new so I didn't have an attachment. Paul Smith isn't gay, but he reminds of Sir James. He is a frequent visitor to different places. At the Auckland Town Hall concerts, he sits two rows behind me. I suddenly miss my home. I have been on the road for almost three weeks. Sometimes I don't get it. If that makes sense, I am a home-loving, adventurous gypsy. Last year, I spent a month in Tokyo. Every year, I return to Tokyo to visit my friends and breathe in the city that is my favorite. I was almost overwhelmed by the fact that I was there for a month. I was sad to leave home towards the end. After Rembrandt and Anne Frank, yesterday I stayed in my hotel room and hibernated. That was exactly what I needed. It makes me feel normal again, and it's a nice break from sightseeing. I also went to bed at 9 o'clock in the morning and slept almost nine hours.

Van Gogh wrote in one of his many letters that he sent to his brother: "I dream of painting, and I paint my dreams." Anne Frank had hoped to be a famous writer. However, she died too soon. My greatest ambition is to make positive changes and make a difference. Before I became tired of the office politics at a women's shelter in Auckland, I was a volunteer for two years. It is not always easy to get a group of intelligent, self-righteous women together in one place. As part of my community service, I taught Chinese at Parnell community center for a time. I was almost a Rotarian. One of my neighbors is a founding member for their local chapter. It was so old-fashioned that I decided to not join the club in the end. Amnesty International will be my next stop when I return to Auckland. I have the chairman in my Auckland Philharmonia Orchestra circle.

They gave us an egg sandwich on the plane and then a small cupcake. They were both very good. Even though I did not allow him to cut into the line earlier, the young man sitting on my left helped with my luggage. My suitcase was lifted by the young father to my right. His little girl would sometimes sit on his lap and kick my knees. It was a three-hour flight.

Writing made it more bearable. After landing in Madrid I took a taxi to get to my hotel. I was able to get to my hotel quickly and didn't wait long. For a flat fee of 30 euros, taxis from the airport to the city centre cost only 30 euro. It was so civilized! I was emailed by the hotel the day before, with information about how to get there from the airport. They were very thoughtful!

I discovered some strange creatures in my hotel room. Two swans had been made from towels in my hotel room, just like the cruise ship. I was hungry so I decided to go out for lunch at a Chinese restaurant. I ordered fried noodles, and I asked them to not add MSG. However, when I got my meal I double-checked their knowledge about MSG. They returned it to me and prepared a new plate. They are lovely people! Because I left my iPhone in Amsterdam, I went to a large shopping center nearby and bought an iPhone charging cable. I was exhausted by the end of the day so I just stayed in bed and watched the news.

Day 21: Madrid

I was awakened by a strange noise at 4 AM. It was the rubbish truck. It was a party for the workers! The workers were playing loud music with the rubbish bins banging, and shouting. I was awake within a few minutes. They took almost an hour. I stayed up until 6am, got up at 6am, and had coffee and a chocolate cookie in my room. Then, I watched an English program about a man who survived in the desert and another man who survived in a swamp. I think I was in a better place than them!

After a quick shower I refreshed my journal and waited until 8 o'clock to ring the reception bell. A little girl dressed in her pajamas walked out of a room. I immediately apologized. When I said I wanted to change rooms, she grumbled even more. She replied, "No rooms now, all filled." I asked Romina, another receptionist to help me and she said that Romina would be there at 9:00 AM.

Romina appeared in my bedroom so I returned to my room. Because she knew I was there, she said she would move me after 12pm. I accepted and then went back to my room to watch more TV about a man fighting with the crocodiles. Then I packed up and left Romina my keys.

The cold wind cut me like an axe as soon as I stepped out of the hotel. I was too early again so I went to Zara and purchased a long dress that would cover my naked legs. This dress saved my life! When I arrived at Pueta de Sol (the gate of the sun), I was still half an hours late. However, I discovered another tour and joined them. This was a huge mistake. Although the guide was British and had lived in Madrid for five years, he was merely reciting history from a textbook. Everyone had to listen to him in the cold wind.

According to the guide, Madrid's symbol was the bear at the Plaza. Take a look at all the years! The year I was born, the bear was also born! This bear symbol can be found everywhere in Madrid, on pavements and police cars!

Plaza Mayor was our next stop. There were already many tourists.

We walked by the Guinness Book of Records' oldest restaurant. I explained to the guide that I was going for the flamenco show. I then showed him the address and asked him if he could point it out to us if we were walking near it. He replied that we weren't going to be anywhere near it, but it was near Plaza Mayor. It was right there, and we passed it within 10 minutes. He didn't even notice it. He walked by the flamenco show several times per day, not even realizing it!

We then walked quickly through Mercado San Miguel. It was gourmet heaven! It was gourmet heaven! I wanted to return there for lunch! He took us to the old church, and we began to recite the history. We were all exhausted and cold. He was not being heard by anyone. Because I knew that the end was near, I was thrilled to see Catedral Nuestra Senora de la Almudena. We were taken to a statue by the guide who then recited something from his history textbook that no one was paying attention to. Although he might have mentioned that the city was built upon the rocks the statue was looking at I wasn't sure.

We were then led to climb a hill. It was incredible to see how our bodies responded when we were pushed. We all followed each other slowly, reluctantly, and eventually made it to the top. Although the view was beautiful, I wouldn't choose to climb that hill.

We finally made it to Plaza Orient, which is just across the street from Palacio Real. Theatre Real was our last stop. After a collective sigh, he was paid tips and we ran. He was not happy with the 10 euro I gave him, and I think he should switch jobs. He clearly didn't care about it! I then went back to the market to get more! I first got some berry juice to quench my thirst from walking and wind, then I tried tapas. It was all delicious! I couldn't finish the shrimp and spinach croquettes. The white bait on bread was divine! I had the famous Spanish hot chocolate. It was heaven! !

With a full stomach, and aching feet, I returned to my hotel content. An accordionist was being played by a man at a small square. It was quite atmospheric! Pueta Del Sol was as full of people every day.

Romina, the hotel clerk, had moved my stuff to the #10 room as promised. Although I was worried about the noise, the bed was just 2m from the corridor that was 75cm wide, I was too tired to think about it. I went straight to bed, but it was too difficult to fall asleep! The guests were constantly checking in, so even with the earplugs, the footsteps, laughter and talking were audible. My neighbour also used water to make the wall shake. I tried to fall asleep with the TV on and the music playing, but it was impossible after 10 minutes. I got up to go find Romina.

After hearing my complaint, she asked the staff to calm down and asked me how long I would like to sleep. I replied an hour. It was not guests who were making noises, but staff members who made them. I explained to her about the water, and she agreed to move my rooms again. They were full, she said, and then she showed me "my neighbor". It was actually the hotel laundry and staff kitchen. This explained the water and microwave pings. I was told that the laundry would be done in 8 minutes. She also asked me to wait 5 minutes before I could go to sleep. I agreed to this grumbly and went back to my bedroom.

Finally, I got some sleep and felt human enough to venture out and explore again. Callao was where my hotel was located. There were many shoe shops nearby so I went into one to try on some sandals. They were cute, but not comfortable. Although I wanted to try western boots, I decided to stay sensible. Then, I was back at Plaza Mayor. Hello again, bear! It was much more pleasant this afternoon.

My jacket was too warm for me. I walked past the adorable little square that I had found earlier. I arrived about 30 minutes early for the flamenco performance. After I confirmed my reservation and found my seat, my wanderlust began. Do I want to buy this flamenco gown? It's red, but I don't know when to wear it. ?

The show was about to begin back at the flamenco venue. After a few drinks, I was already full. I ended up with only half a glass. It was stunningly beautiful. Although I didn't know what they were singing, the lyrics of the sad and haunting tunes made me feel so much. But it was the dance everyone had been waiting for. Both the male and female dancers were amazing! I was even able to dance on stage! I was blaming the sangria!

A very irritating little boy kept running between the two of them.

the tables during the show. He went on stage too and jumped up and down madly, almost falling off the stage. Luckily his mum grabbed him just in time. I asked the American girl sitting next to me to take photos and videos for me. She did an excellent job!

Later I went to see the flamenco dress again. Hmmmm.. maybe I should buy a pair of castanets instead. I went into a gallery that had some cool stuff. I almost bought a painting then I remembered I would need an extra wall at home to put it on! Ahhh that plate was very creative too! No no no no no, I shall behave! There was a free concert at Plaza Mayor when I walked by so I sat down and listened to some traditional Spanish folk songs. The elder female singer still had a very powerful and expressive voice. The band was fantastic too. One of the songs only had piano and singing. Beautiful!

There were many illegal stalls selling fake products. Calamari baguette was a popular snack among the locals but not really my thing. Many tapas bars were doing great business. The locals ate late and slept late. It was nearly 9pm but there were still many people around.

I found a supermarket and bought some food for a late dinner. On my way back, I saw a band playing. The music was very pleasant! Back in my room, I couldn't open the wine bottle so I went to ask the receptionist. She said she would try but then an elderly gentleman walked in just at that moment so we asked him. He opened it in 30 seconds.... cheers!

Day 22: Madrid

I got up around 7am and had my breakfast in the room. The yogurt was so yummy! Then 1 spent nearly 3 hours updating my journal. Finally I left for Sorolla Museum around 11 am. I took the subway and found it quite easy to navigate. However, after I got there, I had to ask several people the directions, including an elderly well-dressed couple, the wife was Japanese and the husband was Spanish.

The neighbourhood was lovely. Finally I found the museum. It was beautiful and the garden was a pure delight! I was so impressed with Sorolla's pottery collection. I spent almost half an hour checking the pottery, then went to his house where the museum was.

The garden was bigger than I first thought. Sorolla probably needed a few gardeners! He painted his family a lot. The first room had a marvelous nude painting of his beloved wife. My favourite was the one with his wife and their new-born daughter.

His studio was stunning too. The view of his studio from another room upstairs was amazing. I spent nearly two hours there.

I was going to take the subway to Prado Museum, but when I asked a girl at the subway station to help me buy the ticket, she took me outside and pointed at the coming bus and gestured to me that I should just jump on. So I did. From the bus I watched her walking back down to the subway but I couldn't thank her... she saved me at least half an hour! After I bought the museum ticket, I had a late lunch at the museum cafe. The cheese and ham sandwich was ok but I really enjoyed the green salad. I also loved the fresh juice. It was quite cold sitting in the shade so I finished my lunch quickly.

Then I went into the museum, three floors of masterpieces! My favourites were of course Maja. The naked Maja was breathtaking.

Goya was such a great storyteller. He had a great sense of humour, too. This painting, Wedding, was the proof. He was probably laughing himself silly working on it! Hilarious painting, hilarious man! Comics are now commonly used to express political views but Goya was certainly a pioneer. Many of his paintings had dogs. He must have been a dog lover!

After the museum, I went to find Crystal Palace in the park. Autumn was there. After almost half an hour of searching in the huge park, I finally found it! Unfortunately, it was under renovation although I could still imagine the glamour. There were many people taking pics there.

On my way to the subway, I saw a magnificent monument, also under renovation. Many people were rowing boats in the lake. It was such a beautiful park. No wonder there were so many people! I walked past the impressive Independence Square on my way to the subway station.

It was almost 3:30pm when I got back to the hotel. I edited the photos that I took today and did the online check-in for my flight the next day. Then I asked Romina to print out the boarding pass for me and ordered me a taxi to the airport. After that I went out to the 9th floor of a nearby building. There were many restaurants there and the view was spectacular. I bought some vegetable noodles and a salad then went to the supermarket in the basement and got some more food. This cinema across from my hotel was probably quite new. I saw quite a few locals having their photos taken in front of it.

Back in my room, I had my interesting dinner! I definitely bought too much... I had about 95% of the meat and cheese... I updated my journal and half watched a programme, 'What On Earth,' about some intriguing mysteries in the world. Then I started packing. I managed to squeeze everything into my little suitcase and the new backpack. Miracles do happen sometimes!

Day 23: Lisbon

Someone was either leaving or arriving around 2am the night before and it woke me up. The previous night, I woke up around the same time too, from the panting and moaning a couple were making next door. This hotel was the worst I had ever stayed in and I was very glad that I was leaving! The alarm woke me at 6am, then I had some pastry, pineapple and coffee for breakfast in my room.

Lisbon was my next stop. I was kind of glad that it would be my last city in

Europe. I was tired of travelling and I missed my baby grand. When I planned this trip, I already knew it would be more educational than recreational. I also knew that it would be a tough journey with so much to learn. I was not sure whether I could do it physically. However, my curiosity won in the end and there I was, one week to go! Having said that, I was enjoying it most of the time - except when I was trip weary of course. According to the weather forecast, Lisbon would be sunny and warm that day and the next couple days too. I liked it already!

Yesterday I asked Romina to book a taxi for me to the airport. The taxi arrived on time this morning. The meter said 30 euro, the official fixed rate. My hotel reminded me that again the day before. (The taxi I took from the airport to my hotel charged me 30 euro too.) The government set the fixed rate for all the airport taxis. However, when I got to the airport, the driver waited till I gave him my credit card and charged me 5 euro extra for a hotel booking fee. I argued that the fixed rate was 30 euro so he showed me a plastic sheet of information in English explaining the maximum for the hotel booking fee in the city of Madrid was 5 euro. I ended up paying 35 euro but I was not happy about that so I asked him to give me that plastic sheet again so that I could take a photo.

To that he replied 'no English'. He then went to the trunk to get my suitcase and pointed at his watch and gestured me to get out so I had no choice but to do what he said. However, I took a photo of him and his taxi and later emailed my hotel to complain about him. I also wrote a review on TripAdvisor. It was not about money. It was about principles.

Later when I was walking to my gate, an elderly gentleman stopped me and tried to tell me something about the taxi this morning. I guessed that he must have witnessed my argument with the taxi driver earlier but I couldn't understand him. After several tries, we finally found a couple who could speak both English and Spanish to translate for us. The gentleman was trying to explain the taxi fare depended on where my hotel was so I told them the whole unpleasant episode and all the Spaniards agreed that the taxi driver was indeed a crook!

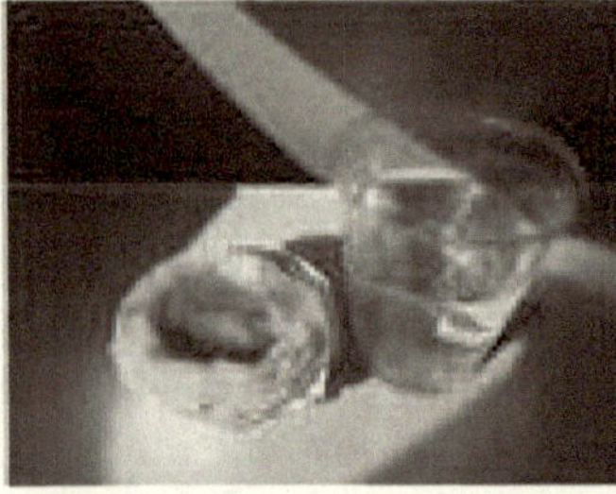

At airport security, I went through smoothly. I had all my cream bottles in a big zipper bag. Success! The sunrise at the airport was beautiful! On the plane, they served us the world famous Portuguese custard tart. Yum yum yum! It was a short taxi ride from the airport to my hotel in the old town. My room was lovely and the view was spectacular.

I asked the hotel for lunch options and they recommended a local restaurant that was just around the corner. I ordered seafood spaghetti paella. It was delicious!

After a nap, I went to find the castle. I took the lift to the top but still had to climb quite a bit. In the end I felt like a goat. However, all the climbing was well worth it. The castle was breathtaking and the view stunning! Some trees in the garden grew peacocks...

After the castle, I walked down the hill and saw a cute little souvenir shop. At a corner I found an outdoor cafe. I sat down and ordered an orange juice. It was a hot day.

A band was playing nearby and the sea breeze was very pleasant. Then I continued my walk back to the hotel. On the way I saw lovely trams running on the road but decided to stay on my feet and continued to explore.

I went into a majestic cathedral and later checked some shops and bought a tile painted with a fado singer. Then I saw a magnificent plaza behind a beautiful gate. Many people were sitting at the beach. It was getting dark so I kept on walking. The shopping street was full of people. I had a take away dinner from an Indian restaurant next to the hotel. Very delicious!

Day 24: Lisbon

The people staying upstairs woke me up around 4am. From the banging and running, I believe they were rushing to the airport. However, they were catcalling too! They were probably still high from their all night partying! Lisbon was so cheap that many young people could afford to come here to party. I had a banana for breakfast then took a cab to Luiz de Camoes plaza for the city tour. The taxi fare was only 5 euro! I was early so I went to a bakery nearby and bought a custard tart.

At 10am, the tour started. Our guide, Jiame, was born in Lisbon but studied in London. Luis de Camoes was a poet who saved his manuscript instead of his Macau girlfriend in a shipwreck. This is another poet who was a monk. Chiado Plaza was named after him. In Portuguese, Chiado means squeak. The poet was like a rapper, creating poems upon requests. He talked so much that he lost his voice and started squeaking.

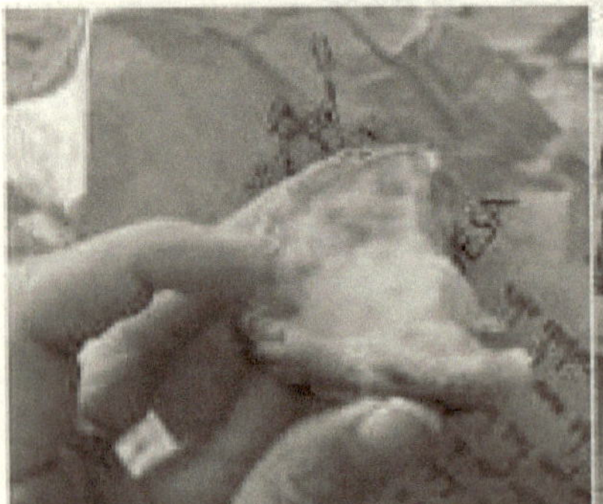

We walked past the oldest bookstore in the world according to the

Guinness Book of Records, although it was probably only true in the west!

Next we went to a convent. The earthquake happened at a big mass on All Saints Day in 1755 and many people died inside. It was supposed to be the best spot to see the castle but we could hardly see anything because of the rain. We were quite a big group.

Later we were taken to see a plaza where they executed people during the inquisition era. Religions are worse than organised crime. Then we saw many university freshmen on the street. It was their initiation day. They paraded around the city in their Harry Potter-like uniforms while singing and chanting.

Our last stop was the big plaza I visited yesterday. It wasn't the seaside as I thought! It was a river!! After the tour, I walked back to my hotel and had an octopus rice at the same restaurant I went to yesterday! Superb! After a nap, I just chilled in the room and updated my journal. About two hours later, I felt I should go out and explore, so I ventured out and watched the university freshmen singing. I went shopping next. I walked to August Street and couldn't resist those mouth-watering pastries!

I walked into a cafe and ordered a cinnamon pastry and a decaf latte. I then stood at the counter having my pastry and coffee just like the locals! On my way out, I bought another pastry for the next day's breakfast. I did some more window-shopping but didn't buy anything else. Such a good girl!

What does one drink in Portugal? Of course port! I had to buy a mini bottle of port. I asked for the best and paid 4 euro for it. Then I went back to the hotel and waited for my ride to the fado show. The driver picked me up at 7:40pm even though he said it would be between 7:45pm and 8pm. He told me there would be a group of 3 and another group of 2 to join me. Since I was the first one, I was allowed to choose my seat. The van had 2 back rows and each had 3 seats. I settled down on one of the two front seats next to the driver. Then we went to pick up the first group. 5 Italians filed in, instead of 3, so the youngest of them, a girl in her early 20s, came and sat next to me. I reluctantly moved to the middle seat from my window seat. Next we went to pick up the group of 2 women in another hotel. However, they were nowhere to be seen when we got there so we had to wait.

While waiting, one of the Italians, the oldest and the biggest, decided to sit next to me so he ordered his granddaughter to swap seats with him. I was horrified when he climbed in beside me. I had no room to move even an inch. My right thigh was squashed against his left thigh and my right arm was touching his left arm. I was extremely uncomfortable.

After about 15 minutes, the two women finally showed up and now the van was jam-packed. As we were about to drive away, I stopped the driver and told him I wanted to swap seats with someone at the back.

He asked the Italian group and finally the granddaughter swapped seats with me. After everybody was happy, we set out to our first stop, a viewpoint up on the hill. The view was not very impressive to be honest but it was nice of him to try.

It was about 9pm when we arrived at the fado club, Guitarrras de Lisboa. It was full! The club had two rooms. There was a big group of tourists in the bigger room. They were squeezed side by side at two very long tables. Something smelled delicious. They were just finishing their first course. Our group got the last table in the adjacent smaller room. I asked the guy who looked like the restaurant owner where the stage was and he pointed at a corner of the big room. I was dismayed because our group would not be able to see anything! I asked if he could move our table but he shrugged his shoulders and said it was a full house. Yeah I could see that alright. Next we were squeezed into our table.

As soon as we sat down, the lights dimmed and the fado show started. Yep, we couldn't see a thing, except every 5 minutes or so, the singer would turn to our direction and gave us 30 seconds of her attention. She was young, beautiful and sounded very good but not only couldn't we see her, we could hardly hear her as well! While she was singing, they gave us some olives, chorizo, spread, bread and lots of wine. I proposed a toast at our table. Then our first course was served. I couldn't really tell what it was because we had to eat in the dark. It was something soupy.

When the singer finished, the lights came back on and they served the big room their main course while we waited. The Italians in our group included an elderly couple from Napoli, their granddaughter and their good friends, plus another couple from Milan. The two women were from South America. The one from Brazil could speak some English.

The other one was from Buenos Aires. They were very interested in my onemonth European trip. We managed to communicate without a common language. Next thing we knew, the light dimmed again because the big group had finished their main course and the second set of the show started. The singer this time was a black widow. Her 4 songs were not very happy. While she was singing, our main course arrived so, again, we had to imagine what we were eating. I thought there was fish, prawns and potato but the rest I wasn't quite sure.

When the black widow finished her weepy songs, we also finished our main course and then the lights came back on because the big room was ready for their dessert. Our group began to feel mistreated so the Brazilian woman had a chat with the waiter. He promised us that the third singer would sing in our room but unfortunately we still had to eat in the dark. He also told us that it was our driver's fault that we had arrived late. A few minutes later, the light dimmed and our dessert was served while the third singer, a robust lesbian, was singing - again in the big room! We were bitterly disappointed but we had our dessert to keep us occupied. The wine helped too.

When the lesbian finished her set, the lights came back on and the people in the big room started leaving. We were just finishing our dessert when the owner of the restaurant decided to turn his club into karaoke and started singing himself. Every note he uttered was completely out of tune.

By then most people were too drunk to care so when he invited us to join in to sing the chorus, most people obliged happily. He 'sang' (I couldn't really call that singing) 3 songs, all the tunes were familiar to the audience who were mostly Portuguese/Spanish/Italian. I could only tell the tunes properly when the audience was singing too. He should have paid us for listening to him, not the other way around! When all the people in the big room left, our group was itching to go too but they drew the curtains closed between the two rooms, moved the musicians into our room and brought the first singer back! We got 2 extra songs!! We almost wept!!!

One elder Italian lady in our group was so pleased that she went and hugged the singer afterwards. She was plastered, even though her granddaughter tried (and failed) many times to stop her from topping up her glass. In the car, the Brazilian woman complained to the driver and he told us that the club always asked him to arrive at 9pm so he was not late at all. He said the club was poorly organised, but I told him it was actually perfectly organised for them to maximise profit. The kitchen couldn't have possibly served all the people at the same time and they didn't have a room big enough to accommodate everyone! Then the driver said his company, the well-known tour operator, Viator, was not to be blamed because it was the club's fault. I replied that it was partially his company's fault because they chose the club for the tour. Everybody in our group agreed. We later exchanged email addresses and promised each other to write our reviews on TripAdvisor.

I enjoyed the singing tonight (the singing of the professional singers that is) but what made this evening memorable was sharing it with some genuine, lovely people!

Day 25: Lisbon

I finally got up around 7:30am. It was a very late night the previous day! I had half of the pastry I had bought the day before and a banana for breakfast. Then I went to catch the tram to the monastery. The tram ticket machine was out of order so I couldn't get a ticket. It took about half an hour to get there. There was a long line there already, even though it was only 9:40am, 20 minutes before they opened! It was definitely worth the wait though. It was simply magnificent!

The church was breathtaking too, but I suddenly remembered the

inquisition era and the evil power of the religions that our guide told us about yesterday. Later I went through the history exhibition there and, to my surprise, quite enjoyed it. The line outside the monastery grew even longer. I even had to queue up to exit! There were many big tours.

Then I walked towards the tram stop but on my way I saw this pastry shop so I joined another queue and had the best custard tart ever! Their spring roll was not bad either!! On the tram back, I failed to buy a ticket again because I didn't have any 5 euro bills or enough coins. It was around 1am that I finally got back to the hotel. I went straight to bed and had a nap. Afterwards I felt much better, so I went to the same restaurant and had grilled sardines for lunch. On my way back to the hotel, I again walked past the shop that had a creepy display in their window. The entrance to my hotel wasn't the most welcoming. One had to climb up a long staircase first!

My dinner was a little bottle of cherry liquor. I was so tired that I skipped a museum in the afternoon and stayed in my room resting. I didn't even have the energy to go out for dinner either. Besides, I wasn't hungry at all, so I just watched some movies in my room in the evening and went to bed around 8:30pm.

Day 26: Marrakech

I woke up around 4:45am, before my 5am alarm. I had had about 8 hours of sleep but I still felt sleepy. Sigh... after this trip I would probably need a month at home to get over the accumulated fatigue! After breakfast, which consisted of a sweet juicy peach and half of the pastry from the day before, I had a quick shower and got ready for my taxi ride to the airport. The driver arrived on time. It took us only 15 minutes to get to the airport. However, there was a long queue at security. Luckily I waited for only about 20 minutes. When I left immigration, the queue was incredibly long - at least 2,000 people were waiting! I was so glad I had got there early. Later I saw a shop selling sardine tins, which didn't seem to be busy at all, well, everybody was queuing up in immigration!

An hour and half later, we landed in Marrakech. There was another long queue at security. I was sick and tired of queuing! They asked us to fill in the disembarkation card before queuing. Luckily I had a pen in my bag. After I finished, a guy asked to borrow my pen, but that would have meant an extra half an hour of queuing to wait for him. Watching the queue quickly getting longer and longer, I had to say no. About 45 minutes later, I finally got out of the airport (after changing 40 euro) and stepped onto the soil of Africa for the first time in my life! My driver from the riad (hotel) was waiting for me outside.

On the way to the riad in the taxi, I experienced culture shock. The horses that were running along the street pulling heavy carts along with cars and motorcycles, the smell of manure, the poor condition of the houses and all the different noises, made me realise Morocco was not only my first African and Muslim country, it was also an entirely different world.

The taxi driver could speak English so we chatted. He told me that he had waited for me for an hour at the airport. Oh yes, the security check at Marrakech airport was notorious. I later gave him a good tip for the wait. He dropped me off at the taxi stand near my hotel. A man was waiting for me there with a cart to carry my luggage to the hotel where cars couldn't reach. I followed the man with my luggage. It took only about 3 minutes but I had another culture shock as I picked my way carefully through potholes and animal dung. The market we walked passed had all sorts of stuff including fruit and vegetables, some of them rotten. The smell, the noise and the strong sun made me feel dizzy. I tipped the cart guy and checked into my riad.

Didi the owner and Adil the manager welcomed me with some pastries and mint tea. Adil joined me for tea and told me the history of this beautiful riad. I was exhausted, but I listened on. Then he took me around to see the riad. Their breakfast was served on the rooftop terrace.

Outside my room, there was a pool. I was pleasantly surprised when I saw my exotic room. There was even a dining area and the bathroom was lovely. I found more pastries in the room but I was all sweetened out! There were many rose petals on the bed and in the bathroom too. However, there was no carpet or tiles on the floor. I was standing directly on concrete. Having said that, I was sure that my hotel was much better than all the low huts I saw on my way that most of the locals lived in. After unpacking, I set my alarm for a 20-minute nap but two girls decided to come to the pool outside my room for a dip just as I started to drift off to sleep. They were trying to be quiet but unfortunately I could hear everything, including the water splashing and their whispers and giggles.

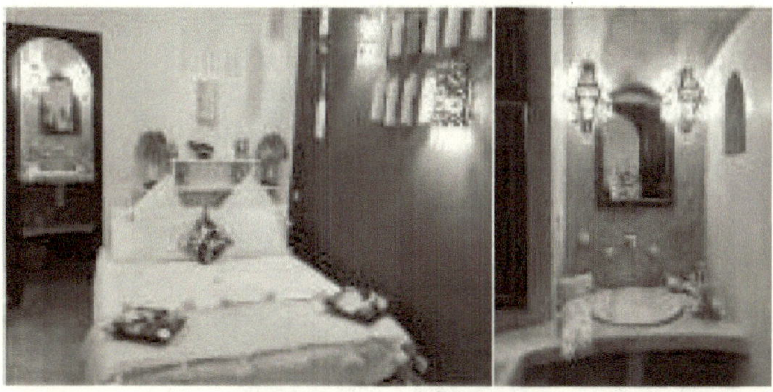

When the alarm went off, I got up reluctantly and got ready for the walk to the market with Adil. It was about 10 minutes there and another 10 minutes back. I had asked him to show me the way to the market. There were many small, nameless allies in the old town. I bought my lunch on the way back. At the entrance to the riad, we met my afternoon guide, Narradine. Adil set the table for my lunch and I ate the yummy chicken while talking to my guide.

That afternoon, Narradine showed me around in the city. He was wearing an official tour guide badge. In Marrakech, only an official guide was allowed to accompany tourists. The police were watching carefully.

I only understood why much later.

After lunch, the tour started. There were many cats around. Didi, the riad owner, later told me the cats there were to catch the rats. Dogs were generally useless, so nobody kept dogs there! I saw a guy selling some strange-looking fruit on the street. Adil told me they were prickly pears. I asked to try one and found it quite sweet and with many seeds, which I spat out on a tissue although the locals apparently swallowed them.

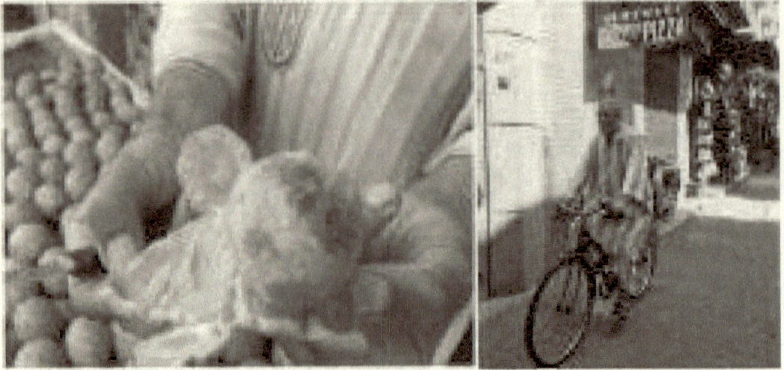

Our first stop was Bias Palace. It was the residence of the prime minister and his many wives. The vivid colour scheme was fascinating! I loved the intricate details of the carving. The tiles were absolutely gorgeous!

Then we walked to the next stop, the Saadian Tombs. There was a covered souk in the Jewish quarter. The Jews had long left but their houses with balconies were still standing. There were many shops selling spices. I loved the smell! Some shops were selling dyes too.

Most of the walls there were red. Adil told me that Marrakech was called the Red City because of those red walls.

The Saadian Tombs were inside a mosque. It was magnificent! I spent a long time admiring all the detail. There was a fabulous gate outside the mosque.

Next we took a taxi to Jardin Majorelle, a lovely garden designed by Yves Saint Laurent. The blue was simply stunning! There were so many cacti there! The yellow and blue were such a beautiful contrast! We left around 4:10pm and waited almost half an hour to get a taxi! Adil told the driver where the riad was then we said good-bye. He was very nice but I didn't think the tour was worth 60 euro. It was around 5pm when I got back to the riad.

I was exhausted! It was lovely to be back at the riad. The sofa right outside my room in front of the pool looked very inviting, but I went back to my room and snoozed. After a shower, I had dinner at the courtyard. Didi the owner and I had a chat. He and his gay partner moved there from Paris 5 years ago. They often visited their friends back in Paris. It was only a 3-hour flight!

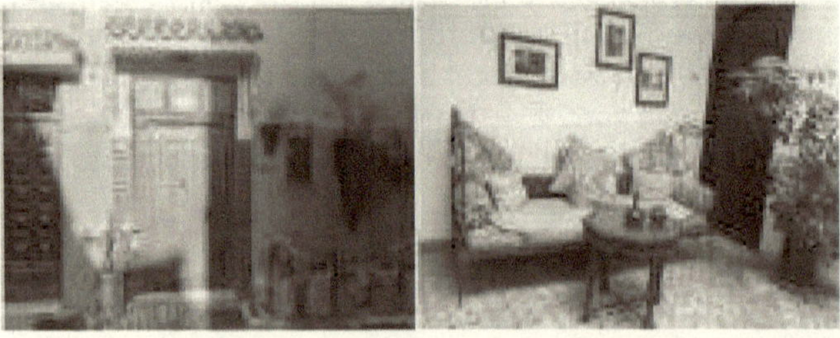

My dinner was served. The first course was some deep-fried stuff...! managed to finish it. But I left the bread untouched. The tagine beef was cooked for 3 hours and was simply divine! The dessert was peanut ice cream and fried banana. After dinner, I went straight to bed. A most extraordinary day!

Day 27: Marrakech

I woke up around 6am, to the prayer call on the PA system! Reluctantly I got up, not to pray but to get ready for my excursion. Breakfast was on the rooftop terrace. It was freezing up there!

My guide, also called Adil, picked me up right on time. Our first stop was a camel ride! Braham helped me to get on Shakira the camel. I looked tiny with my new best friend! I had mint tea afterwards.

I saw many pottery shops on the way, so I asked Adil to take me to one. I have been playing with mud for over 5 years now. Back at home, I have a collection of wonky cups. The pottery shop Adi chose was huge.

It was also a studio/factory. The pots there were all very dirty. Adil cleaned some of them so that I could pick one. Finally I chose a dark blue one.

Next we went to a market. This building outside the market was stunning! There were only men in the market, apart from the female tourists of course. I was the only adult woman there that day. Berber women stayed home and looked after the children and animals. There were all sorts of stalls.

The smell from the food stalls was wonderful! Adil took me to a deep-fried sardine shop. He bought us each a sardine sandwich. I had some eggplant and chilly in mine. Wow! I could get addicted to this! Adil later had to go back and bought himself another one! Following Adil's advice, I bought some notebooks for the village children.

Then we set out to our next destination, the village. There were many resorts on the way along the river. Argon Oil Corporative was for divorced or widowed women. They were lovely ladies but their work was extremely labour intensive.

With their encouragement, I gave it a go. Hmmm... Definitely not for me!

Later, one of the women took me upstairs and introduced their products. It was embarrassing because I didn't have enough cash for a bottle of oil. I had to change my plan and bought a perfume rock instead.

After we got back in the car, Adil and I had a chat. I was surprised when he told me that he was 44. He looked so young! He had an 1 lyo son who he met every two weeks because of his job. Finally we were up in the mountains! The children were so happy to receive the notebooks from me. They ran to me and left with such beautiful smiles. Their smiles were worth 1,000 times more than my investment!

Adil stopped the car very often to smoke. He got some water from a spring. I tasted some of the cold clear water. It was delicious! After about an hour on the winding road, I became carsick. I was so relieved when we finally reached the lunch place. It was a gorgeous village house. The cook was making bread when we arrived.

The view of the mountains was soothing. They prepared some mint tea for my stomach but what really saved me was the Coca Cola that Adil asked his colleague to bring me later! When I felt a bit better, they served us lunch. I loved the salad although I didn't have much appetite. The chicken tagine was tasty and the couscous was also very delicious!

The dessert was an apple. Adil told me to take it away and eat it later. It was such a lovely lunch. It was a real shame that my stomach was not well! We made one more stop so Adil could smoke. It was around 4pm when we made it back to my riad. I went straight to bed.

After a nap, I went to Ben Youssef Madrasa. I saw a little sheep walking on the street too. Then I found a beautiful building and thought it was Ben Youssef Madrasa but actually it was his museum. I loved the light green colour! On my way back to the riad, I got completely lost and as a result, found the real Ben Youssef Madrasa by mistake! It was a magnificent building! I got there 10 minutes before closing but there were still many people inside! I was fascinated by the beautiful roof window!

Finally I found my way back to the riad and had a massage at 8pm, the perfect ending to a wonderful day! I slept like a baby that night!!

Day 28: Marrakech

Again, I was woken up by the prayer call at 6am. I had the apple I got the day before and updated my journal. After a shower and a shampoo (my hair was oily from the massage so I had to wash it again!), I went upstairs for breakfast. They made the egg for me at my request.

Then I rushed off to Cafe de France, the meeting place for my cooking class. I was there a little early. Karima, the chef, got there right on time. A group of 6 Americans came a bit later. First we went to the souk to get the ingredients. I asked Karima not to show us the chickens being killed. All the other people agreed, so we bought the frozen chicken from the day before. All the cats there were eating chicken. It was quite a disturbing sight for some reason.

The riad where we had the cooking class was lovely. Karima was the manager and chef there. Everything in the riad was gorgeous. She showed us how to make mint tea. Then we started cooking chicken tagine. The bell peppers were roasted on an open fire. After all the chopping, we mixed the ingredients in tagine pots and put the pots directly on the fire. Next we prepared salad and did some more chopping. While waiting for the chicken, we chatted and had some more tea. The Americans were there for their friends' wedding.

Lunch was a proper 3-course feast. The salad was divine. I almost finished the whole chicken tagine myself! The dessert was orange and grape but the cinnamon completely transformed the taste. Yum!!

Finally, we went back to the square and said good-bye. Then I went to the ATM before meeting my souk guide at Cafe de France. The locals had just finished their prayer. My guide Redu was very fat. I disliked him immediately because he was not only late but had a very strange way of looking at people. He seemed to know everybody although they all called him Azik. I told him I wanted to buy a dress and he took me to a lamp shop that happened to have some dresses. I picked a dress and the shop owner gave me a ridiculous price, 80 euros. I was about to put it down when he said 40. I decided to leave the shop, which made him very angry and told me not to return, to that I happily obliged. I stopped trusting Redu after that.

The second shop he took me to was a tagine shop and I didn't buy anything. The third shop he took me to sold carpets. I didn't buy any either. I walked away from a tagine pot and a carpet I liked because I knew the prices were outrageous. Later I decided to walk into a shop at random and found the same dress that I liked in the first shop. The owner asked 40 euros for it so I said 15. In the end we settled for 20! The first shop asked for 80!! Redu was such a prick!!! Finally I asked him to take me to the carpet shop that I had found online and he reluctantly did. It was a pity that I couldn't find anything I liked there. Their prices were much more reasonable.

After the carpet shop, Redu gave up on making any commission from me, even though I had already paid 35 euros online for his 4-hour service. He took me to the plaza and ended the tour 2 hours early. I didn't protest because I was only too happy to get rid of him. I thanked him (for nothing) then went shopping on my own. I managed to find a beautiful long dress, but soon got tired. It had been a long day!

On my way back to the riad, I was lost and a young guy offered to show me the way. I refused, but he walked very fast so that I couldn't stop him. When we got to my riad, he asked for money and I said no. He then spat on me!!! I just carried on walking, although feeling nauseous, and went into my riad. Apparently many young local men waited around and when they saw tourists, they initiated conversation and asked where they were going. OK my sense of direction was appalling, but I knew it was not just me. Many tourists in the old town of Marrakech were constantly lost. There were simply too many small alleys and side streets going in all directions.

When the lost and desperate tourists found someone local who offered to help, they were so relieved and grateful that they accepted only too willingly. That was how the local young men found their prey. They walked fast in front of the tourists while keeping a distance to avoid being caught by the police. These guys of course didn't have the official tour guide badges. While 'guiding,' they looked back frequently to make sure the tourists were following. When they reached the destination, usually less than 5 minutes away but impossible for the tourists to find on their own, they asked for money. Sometimes they offered to help even when the tourists didn't need any help, and then they asked for money later anyway. I had two men volunteer to 'help' me to find my way during my 3-day stay. The first guy only grumbled when I refused to pay, but the guy today not only spat on me, but also used the f word. It was most unpleasant.

After I got back, I paid the riad cash for my stay, the taxi, a dinner and a massage. Then I ordered another massage because I had hardly spent any money shopping this afternoon! Later in my room, I tried on my new dress! Gorgeous!!

I was so unprepared for Marrakech even though I had done my homework. I knew it was not safe for single female tourists to be travelling alone here, so I booked 4 tours for my 3-day stay so that someone would always accompany me. However, it was still unavoidable to be alone sometimes. My first tour guide was nice but quite boring. Reading a history textbook myself would have been more interesting! My second guide was the best. He took me to some Berber villages in the mountains. I got to meet the real people in their homes. I was usually the only tourist around. On my last day, I had a cooking class in the morning with a fantastic local teacher and a group of American tourists. We first went to the souk to get the food, then cooked chicken tagine together. In the afternoon, I had another private tour guide taking me shopping in the souk. Unfortunately, he was not only late but also too fat and too lazy to move. All the shops he took me to were dodgy.

Having said all that, Marrakech was certainly not the only place in the world that had crooks and scammers. The fact that it was a 3rd world country had nothing to do with it either. I would still like to believe that most locals in Marrakech were kind. For example, I met these two older gentlemen the morning I tried to find my way to the square, the meeting place for the cooking class. They were wearing something quite shabby but clean, and spoke no English. In fact, they couldn't read at all. It was around 8:30am and they were the only people around so I pointed at the square on my map that was in their language, but they shook their heads. They only realised where I wanted to go when I tried to pronounce the name of the square. They started walking ahead of me and gestured me to follow at a distance. They made sure I got to the square safely. Maybe I am being stubborn and silly now, but the shy smile they gave me when we parted is the Marrakech I choose to remember.

I enjoyed my Marrakech experience but I don’t think I would go back anytime soon!

Day 29: Rome

The morning call from the mosque woke me up before 6am again but I struggled to get up. Finally I made myself crawl out of the bed and went to the courtyard to find my breakfast. However, nobody was there so I knocked on the night manager's door and woke him up. I explained that I was told to have breakfast at 6:30am in the courtyard. He said ok.

He served me breakfast after he told me that he was told to give me breakfast at 7:30am... well anyway I had a nice breakfast and then I thanked him, went back to my room, had a shower and finished my packing just in time for the taxi. Following the same routine, a guy was waiting for me outside with a cart. He put my suitcase in the cart then we walked for about 5 minutes when I saw the driver waiting for me, the same one who had picked me up at the airport.

On my way to the airport, I told the driver about the guy who spat on me the day before, and he told me he would look after me next time... It was about 8:30am when we arrived at the airport, 2 hours before my flight. However, there was a long queue outside waiting to enter the airport! It was the first security check.

I was dismayed and worried. I asked a guy in front of me what was going on and he said it would be ok. It turned out that he was taking the same flight. He was from Rome. After I cleared the first security check, I walked straight to boarding but was told to get my boarding pass stamped first, even though I had checked in online already.

I walked back to the lobby and ran into the Italian guy there. Together we spent nearly half an hour running back and forth trying to locate the counter to get the stamp. Eventually we found the counter and got our boarding passes stamped, then we went to the boarding area, cleared the second security check and passport control. I was sweating like a piglet by the time we finally reached the gate. Hang on, do piglets sweat?

While waiting to board, we relaxed and chatted. He was a medical technician in Rome and was in Morocco on holiday. He showed me some photos of camels and the desert he had been to. I also showed him my camel and the desserts I had eaten! Our flight was full of screaming babies. He asked me to look after his luggage and ran to the toilet. When he came back, he told me that he had an upset stomach...

After we boarded, I found my window seat easily but I had to walk past a Moroccan woman and her daughter. She asked if I could swap my seat with her mum who was sitting on the aisle seat next to them. I was too nice... I said yes against my better judgment. It turned out to be a very bad decision.

My neighbours, two Italian mums, had to go to the toilet later and they didn't go together. Instead they went one after another. Then one of them wanted to swap seats with another woman in their group so I had to make space for them. I asked the woman at the window seat if she wanted to swap seats with me, but she preferred a window seat. Her son and daughter kept coming to talk to her. An hour later, her daughter decided that she wanted to sit with mum after all so, again, I had to let them do the swap. On top of that, there was a screaming baby with a pair of extremely healthy lungs. The worst thing for me, however, was the BOs. OMG!!!

3 hours later when we landed, there was a sudden jolt and a violent shake. I grabbed the back of the seat in front of me, probably whitefaced, while a round of applause exploded around me from the relieved passengers. I only chose Ryanair because this flight was the only direct flight from Marrakech to Rome that day. I will never fly with them again!

After we got off the plane, the Italian guy and I exchanged names and now we are FB friends! His name is Quintilio. My taxi driver was waiting for me outside. I was so exhausted that I almost fell asleep in the cab. I managed to stay awake only because the driver was texting all the way, which kept me quite alert.

Half an hour later, I checked into my hotel but had to ask to swap rooms because the first room was right at the hotel entrance even though it faced the courtyard. The second room, Room 204, faced the street but it wasn't too bad with the window closed. I tried to have a snooze but was too hungry, so I got up and asked Bruno at the front desk to recommend a restaurant. He recommended the one across from us so I went.

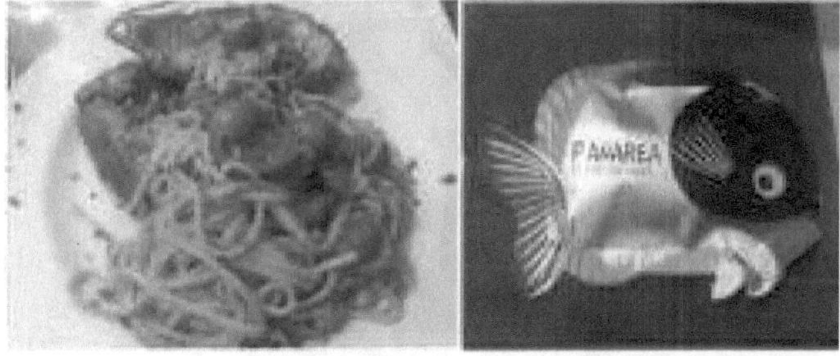

The calamari was cooked perfectly, very tasty and tender. The salad was fresh but nothing spectacular. They gave me free champagne! I was still hungry so I ordered lobster linguini. Yum yum yum! I couldn't finish everything but my stomach was finally happy. The wet towel in a fish shape package was very cute!

It was about 5pm when I finished my late lunch/early dinner. I went back to my hotel room and updated my journal. There were many restaurants outside, but the noise from the diners didn't bother me. What upset me was the Italian guy next door. He banged everything loudly and screamed into the phone. I had to turn up my TV volume to cover his noise!

Day 30: Rome

I slept till about 7:30am. I must have been exhausted. I slowly got ready and drank lots of water. Then I set out to find some breakfast. It was too cold so I had to go back to my room to change into jeans and a jacket. Then I thought I would just have breakfast at the shopping district but on my way to the subway, I saw a bakery so I went in and got myself a pastry and a coffee. The pastry was too sweet so I didn't finish it.

I took the subway to Piazza Poppula and asked a girl how to get to the famous shopping street. Of course she knew what I was talking about! On my way there, there was a flea market but I didn't stay.

The plaza was huge. Most people were walking in the same direction to the shops. Our destination was the same! It was a bit weird to see the armed police with a tank there though. I bought lots of dresses and 3 hours later I was tired, so I took a taxi back to the hotel and dropped off my shopping.

Then I went to the same restaurant for lunch and ordered lasagna. The restaurant had quickly become my favourite there! I wore one of my new dresses to lunch, then I changed into another new dress to the ballet, Giselle.

The theatre was only 5 minute away on foot. It was such a treat! I was in tears when Giselle saved her lover's life. Talk about unconditional love! Then I went to a nearby Chinese restaurant for dinner. I had beef and lettuce. Yum! On my way back to the hotel, I bought a beer and had it in my room. Life is good!!

Day 31: Rome

My last day of the trip! I am so looking forward to flying home even though I am really not looking forward to the flying itself. It was very noisy here last night. My neighbours came back and talked loudly, the diners downstairs sang, and the rubbish truck came. I finally got up around 7:30am and then had a banana and a gigantic peach for breakfast.

Eugene picked me up around 9:40am and we went to his farm. It took us over 2 hours to get there! We stopped at a supermarket to get some frozen prawns and mushrooms. His farm was very basic but the view was spectacular! Then Eugene made lunch while I played with Tiger the cat. He was very friendly but a bit violent when playing. I was scratched and the doctor disinfected my finger right away. After lunch, it took us another 2 hours to get back to Rome. It was about 4pm when Eugene dropped me off.

I came back to the safety of my room, packed and then had a nap. Later around 6:30pm, I went out to find dinner. I bought a bottle of water, a beer and Indian take-away! I watched ER while having my dinner. George Clooney was so young then! Wow!! I think he looks more delicious than my dinner!!!

I left home a month ago and I am finally going home tomorrow. Home sweet home! It was a wonderful trip, an adventure in fact. I took myself outside my comfort zone and explored the unknown. As we get older, we tend to stay with what we know but I think it's necessary to venture into uncharted territory, meet wonderful people and experience different cultures. One month was a long time away from home travelling on my own but I am glad I did.

To me, this trip is like visiting my old composer friends even though all of them are long dead! However, their music is a big part of me and I feel strangely connected to them. I believe they have had a significant influence on my life including how I think and how I feel. I love the European arts and architecture too but I can't say they move me in the same way as European music.

Yes, I am glad that I've done this crazy journey and visited 11 countries in 31 days! Thank you, Beethoven. Thank you, Bach. Thank you, Brahms. Thank you to all the composers that have brought me the joy of my life - music!

www.ingramcontent.com/pod-product-compliance
Lightning Source LLC
LaVergne TN
LVHW091323150826
845673LV00006B/1740